W9-ACK-918

MARK & HELEN OSTERLIN LIBRARY
NORTHWESTERN MICHIGAN COLLEGE
TRAVERSE CITY, MICHIGAN 49686-3061

WITHDRAWN

PLAYBOOKS
and CHECKBOOKS

PLAYBOOKS
and CHECKBOOKS

An Introduction to the
Economics of Modern Sports

Stefan Szymanski

PRINCETON UNIVERSITY PRESS

PRINCETON AND OXFORD

To my family

for their unstinting support

COPYRIGHT © 2009 BY PRINCETON UNIVERSITY PRESS

PUBLISHED BY PRINCETON UNIVERSITY PRESS, 41 WILLIAM STREET,
PRINCETON, NEW JERSEY 08540
IN THE UNITED KINGDOM: PRINCETON UNIVERSITY PRESS,
6 OXFORD STREET, WOODSTOCK, OXFORDSHIRE OX20 1TW
ALL RIGHTS RESERVED

LIBRARY OF CONGRESS
CATALOGING-IN-PUBLICATION DATA
SZYMANSKI, STEFAN, 1960-
PLAYBOOKS AND CHECKBOOKS : AN INTRODUCTION TO THE
ECONOMICS OF MODERN SPORTS / STEFAN SZYMANSKI.
P. CM.
INCLUDES INDEX.
ISBN 978-0-691-12750-7 (CLOTH : ALK. PAPER) 1. PROFESSIONAL
SPORTS—ECONOMIC ASPECTS. 2. SPORTS—ECONOMIC ASPECTS.
3. SPORTS ADMINISTRATION. I. TITLE.
GV716.S993 2009
338.4'779604—DC22   2008041117

BRITISH LIBRARY CATALOGING-IN-PUBLICATION DATA IS AVAILABLE
THIS BOOK HAS BEEN COMPOSED IN JANSON TEXT

PRINTED ON ACID-FREE PAPER. ∞

PRESS.PRINCETON.EDU

PRINTED IN THE UNITED STATES OF AMERICA
1 3 5 7 9 10 8 6 4 2

Contents

Six

Preface

An old joke told in Boston:

On the first day of school a first-grade teacher explains to her class that she is a Yankees fan. She asks her students to raise their hands if they, too, are Yankees fans. Wanting to impress their teacher, everyone in the class raises a hand except one little girl.

The teacher looked at the girl with surprise and said, "Janie, why didn't you raise your hand?"

"Because I'm not a Yankees fan," she replied.

The teacher, shocked, asked, "Well, if you are not a Yankees fan, then who are you a fan of?"

"I am a Red Sox fan, and proud of it," Janie replied.

The teacher could not believe her ears. "Janie, why, pray tell, are you a Red Sox fan?"

"Because my mom is a Red Sox fan, and my dad is Red Sox fan, so I'm a Red Sox fan too!"

"Well," said the teacher in an annoyed tone, "that is no reason for you to be a Red Sox fan. You don't have to be just like your parents all of the time. What if your mom were an idiot and your dad were a moron, what would you be then?"

"Then," Janie smiled, "I'd be a Yankees fan."

No doubt a similar joke is told in New York with the teams reversed. There are websites constructed by Red Sox fans devoted to their hatred of the Yankees. As the winningest team in the history of baseball, the

Yankees have many enemies (hence the popularity of the T-shirt slogan "I support [*your team's name here*] and anyone who beats the Yankees"). However, the rivalry between the Yankees and the Red Sox is something special. It dates back over one hundred years and stems from the antagonism between two of America's greatest and oldest cities. According to *USA Today*, "There's no rivalry in sports that comes close."

The stories have been retold many times. Both teams were formed in the first years of the twentieth century as part of the recently created American League. In 1903 the AL achieved major league status, persuading the older National League to agree to an annual championship between the best team in each league. Boston won the first World Series in 1903 and four more by 1918, becoming the first dominant team of the twentieth century. The New York Yankees by contrast languished as poorer neighbors of the National League's New York Giants, and failed to win an AL pennant in the first twenty years of their existence. The moment that changed the fortunes of these two teams is the greatest legend in baseball.

Harry Frazee, the owner of the Red Sox, was short of cash in 1919, needing money to finance his other interest, which was producing Broadway shows. So he sold a number of players who were causing him problems to his much weaker New York rival, including a young pitcher turned outfielder—Babe Ruth. The Red Sox and the Yankees continued to trade like this for several years, but the influx of players into New York turned the tide of success. Ruth, called the Bambino for his baby-faced looks, transformed baseball with his big hitting and his box-office persona. Soon after Yankee Stadium was opened in 1923, it came to be known as the "House That Ruth Built," because of his drawing power. The team also boasted the talents of Lou Gehrig, arguably the greatest first baseman of all time. With a supporting cast whose power hitting earned them the sobriquet "Murderers' Row," Ruth's Yankees won six pennants and four World Series before his departure in 1934. Meanwhile, the "Curse of the Bambino," as it came to be known, settled over the Red Sox, who failed even to win another pennant until after World War II.

For most of the postwar era the Yankees were successful when the Red Sox struggled and vice versa, but it was the Yankees that took all the honors. In the sixteen seasons from 1947 to 1962, the Yankees took ten World Series, led by Hall of Famers like Joe DiMaggio, Mickey Mantle, Whitey Ford, Yogi Berra, and Roger Maris. In this period the Red Sox managed only one World Series appearance, thanks largely to their batting hero, Ted Williams. Sox fans even came to resent what they see as the baseball public's undervaluation of their hero, which they attribute to the machinations of the Yankee publicity machine.

Starting in 1962 the Yankees suffered under the ownership of the broadcaster CBS, and fared little better when a syndicate led by shipbuilder George Steinbrenner took over in 1973. Meanwhile the Sox produced competitive teams led by Carl Yastrzemski, but still failed to lay the curse to rest. Worst of all was giving up a fourteen-game lead in the 1978 season to the Yankees, including a series of defeats at the hands of the Yankees known as the "Boston massacre," and losing to them in the play-off for the pennant. Of course, the Yankees went on to win another World Series. The Red Sox were the better team in the 1980s, while the Yankees returned to dominance in the

1990s, winning four out of five World Series between 1996 and 2000 (prompting much soul-searching about the decline of competitive balance in baseball).

By the end of 2003 many Red Sox fans must have considered giving up baseball all together. In that season the two teams met in the American League Championship Series once again. In the seventh game the Sox were 5–2 up in the eighth inning, just five outs from winning the series. But with the pitcher tiring and with some poor fielding by the Sox, the Yankees scored three runs, tied the game, and won in extra innings.

The Curse of the Bambino was finally erased in 2004, in the most dramatic fashion possible. This time the Yankees won the first three games in the ALCS, a deficit no team had ever survived in the history of baseball. In game 4 the Yankees were ahead 4–3 in the bottom of the ninth, just three outs from a clean sweep. Amazingly, the Red Sox scored to tie the game, win in extra innings, and then win the series, for the greatest comeback in baseball history. Then the Red Sox swept the World Series, and after a wait of eighty-six years Boston once again had absolute baseball bragging rights over the Big Apple.

Without doubt this rivalry has produced some of the greatest moments in the history of sports, as well as some of the greatest highs for the fans when their team wins. It's not just the skill of the players, but the rivalry itself that produces high drama, remarkable athletic feats but also exceptional errors brought on by pressure. If it were scripted, no one would think it believable. If you could sell it, it would be worth millions. . . .

But imagine for a moment that a Red Sox fan could press a button that would expel the Yankees forever from Major League Baseball. Would he press it? Anyone capable of wearing a T-shirt proclaiming themselves a "Yankee Hater" ($14.99 on the Internet) would be tempted. But in a moment of clarity this fan might realize that without the Yankees to loathe, the pleasure of supporting the Red Sox would be a little bit smaller. Here is the fundamental truth of modern sports—rivalries make for excitement. However much you loathe your rivals, you cannot play without them, and the bigger the rival, the better the game. Now, fans have been known to drink the odd beer, and after a few beers the typical fan might not think twice about pressing the button. Our heads and our hearts, in other words, are not entirely in agreement about this proposition. We follow sports at an emotional level, and feelings dictate what we say and think about sports. But sports competition is the product of rational design. In the modern era an astonishing array of sporting competitions have been created to entertain us, and this book is about how they are designed. This is necessarily a matter of economics, since a sporting competition needs economic resources in the form of skilled labor, equipment, land, and buildings.

That sporting competitions succeed when they create exciting rivalries is the central proposition of the economics of sports. It is not hard to find other examples in baseball (Cubs and Cardinals, Giants and Dodgers), football (Bears and Packers, Texas and Oklahoma) or basketball (Sixers and Celtics, Knicks and Nets). Outside of the United States, the major soccer rivalries dominate the landscape. At the club level the rivalries of Manchester United and Liverpool in England, Barcelona and Real Madrid in Spain, or AC Milan and Internazionale in Italy are as storied as the Red Sox and Yankees, while soccer played at international level fuels nationalistic jealousies

(Brazil and Argentina, Netherlands and Germany, Japan and Korea). Outside of team sports, rivalries between star players also fuel interest in sport. For example, men's tennis has enjoyed a renaissance thanks to the rivalry between Roger Federer and Rafael Nadal; many commentators argue that without it, the sport would still be struggling to retain the interest of fans, which had lagged since the end of the Borg-McEnroe rivalry of the late 1970s and early 1980s. Women's tennis has benefited over the years from the rivalry between Chris Evert and Martina Navratilova, between Steffi Graf and Monica Seles, and in more recent years between the sisters Serena and Venus Williams. In the case of NASCAR it was the fistfight between Cale Yarborough and Donnie Allison after they crashed into each other on the final lap at the Daytona 500 in 1979 that catapulted stock car racing to national prominence. Formula One motor racing has also benefited from great rivalries, between Alain Prost and Ayrton Senna or Michael Schumacher and Damon Hill.

For any organizer of a sporting competition, the most important issue is how to maintain and develop rivalry. In 1999, the Italian Competition Authority ruled that the sale of broadcast rights by Lega Calcio, the Italian soccer league, could no longer be permitted. The authority ruled that collective selling amounted to a restriction of competition, since there were few, if any, sports rights in Italy of similar importance or that were reasonable substitutes. Before this date the league had sold the rights on behalf of the clubs and distributed the money between the teams, a system which is used by most other sports leagues around the world. In the eyes of the Italian Competition Authority, collective selling served only to raise the price at which these rights were sold. The arrangement was deemed in the context of the rules of the game and the setup of the contest, that one can understand the incentives of the athletes. For example, it is common for fans to bewail the absence of pay for performance in team sports, especially when an athlete plays badly. However, the ways players are paid is a consequence of the market for playing talent. Teams that offer to employ stars on performance contracts that expose the player to significant risk will find they have to offer far more in total salaries than teams that offer a fixed amount, regardless of how well the player performs. Thus wages often include an element of "insurance" against the risk of poor performance (as indeed do the wages that most of the rest of us earn). Likewise, the incentives to cheat, through match fixing or taking banned substances, are usually a function of the underlying setup of the competition.

In chapter 5 the role of broadcasting in the development of sport is considered. Broadcasting represented a fundamental revolution in the economics of sports because of the almost unlimited increase in audience size that it permitted (in more or less the same way that sound recording revolutionized the status of performing artists and film revolutionized the status of actors). Chapter 5 examines how the organizers of sporting competitions reacted by changing the design of championships and the way in which the development of technology is likely to continue this process.

Finally, chapter 6 deals with possibly the most interesting relationship in the sports business, the relationship with government. Government participation goes far beyond the role played by the courts in the enforcement of fair competition, and encompasses public subsidies for sports facilities and events, the advancement of regional and national prestige, and the promotion of public health, education, and any number of other benefits, real or imagined, that politicians identify with sports.

This book provides an overview of what I consider to be the main issues in sports economics, so there is no point pretending that it is anything other than a partial view, in both senses of the word *partial*. Many important topics are ignored or sidestepped, and while the beginner's guide to the sports economics literature, found at the end of the book, will let the conscientious reader fill some gaps, I have my own opinions about what matters and what does not. To some extent my personal take is to be found in the epilogue. However, if these final thoughts have any value (and when it comes to barroom opinions, I have to take my turn in line with everyone else), it is only because of the thinking that has gone into the previous six chapters.

A Short Note about Economists

For a discipline that lays some claim to scientific rigor, economics is surprisingly fixated on names and authorities. In my professional career I never cease to be amazed by the frequency with which I hear the assertion, made without any apparent sense of irony, "It must be so because X said so." In this book I have left out detailed references to scholarly work simply to make reading easier, but behind most of my arguments there is scholarly work somewhere (although the reader should feel free to believe everything I say is true just because I say so!). In the beginner's guide at the end of this book I have provided references to some authorities. There undoubtedly are others I have omitted who deserve to be included in a comprehensive review, and to them I can only apologize. In the text a few names crop up, and it is worth taking a moment to introduce the most important of them here.

First, there is Simon Rottenberg, truly the father of sports economics, whose celebrated paper in 1956 resonated with the later and much more famous work of Ronald Coase. Both of these economists believed that competition produces a distribution of resources, while in theory a benevolent and infallible central planner would produce another (optimal) distribution, and the interesting question is how they compare. Second, there is Gordon Tullock, a significant figure in the field of research known as public choice, who first formulated a model of a contest back in the 1960s. This model is so elegant and so insightful that it deserves to be even more widely studied than it is already. Third, there is Walter Neale. Like Rottenberg, he wrote only one notable article about sport, and even that is quite obviously flippant. He coined the memorable phrase "the peculiar economics of sport" and stressed the crucial peculiarity, that participants in a sporting contest may be *sporting* competitors, but are not necessarily *economic* competitors. Sporting competitors may even wish to see their rivals thrive in order to create a better contest. Fourth, there is Gerald Scully, whose 1974 paper demonstrated how it was possible to relate performance of hitters and pitchers in baseball to the revenue generated by a franchise, and thus to show what they were truly "worth," at least in economic terms. As one might expect with pioneering work, it raised as many issues as it settled, but his insight combined with the growth in computing power since then influenced thinking on sports well beyond the groves of academe.

Fifth, there is John Nash, mathematician, economics Nobel Prize winner, and celebrated subject of the book and film *A Beautiful Mind*. Nash's contribution was to explain how to approach almost any economic problem where the decision makers are in competition with each other, or at least not explicitly trying to cooperate. It is not that he made any specific contribution to the study of sports economics, it is just hard to do any economics without considering his insights. Finally, and slightly oddly, there is John Maynard Keynes. As far as I know, he was not remotely interested in sport, but his ideas, or at least a version of them, have been used to justify public expenditure on facilities to host major sports events or professional sports teams. I suspect he would turn in his grave.

PLAYBOOKS

and CHECKBOOKS

One

SPORTS AND BUSINESS

On February 27, 1874, a game of baseball was played at Lord's Cricket Ground in London, between teams led by two men who shaped the destiny of sports across the globe. On one side was a young Al Spalding, founder of the sporting goods company and a man who helped create modern professional baseball. On the other was Charles Alcock, secretary of the prestigious Surrey Cricket Club and of the recently formed Football Association.

Spalding had been sent to London by his team manager to see whether it would be possible to organize a tour of Great Britain to exhibit the brash new American game of baseball. Spalding was to play a prominent role in the creation of the National League two years later, and to steer the professional game through its early years. By the time he wrote *America's National Game* in 1911 it was not only that, but also a significant business enterprise. Alcock, who acted as the London agent for Spalding's 1874 tour and the more famous world tour of 1888–89, instigated international competition in both cricket and soccer and created the first important competition in soccer, the Football Association (FA) Cup. Perhaps even more importantly, he ensured that there was no parting of the ways between amateur and professionals in soccer.

The split between amateur and professional happened early in baseball. The rules of baseball were first written down by Alexander Cartwright of the Knickerbocker

Club of New York in 1845. Their game was one for gentlemen amateurs, a sociable excuse for an evening's eating
and drinking. As the game became popular, enthusiastic
crowds came to watch the amateurs play; commercially
minded players saw an opportunity to sell tickets, and
once the game was an entertainment, teams saw that they
could bring in even more money by fielding the best players. Pretty soon there was a market for baseball talent and
the modern business of baseball was born. In 1871, however, the amateurs declared that they wanted nothing to
do with commercialism, and baseball divided into amateur and professional camps. Ever since, the professional
game has shown almost no interest in the development of
the sport at amateur and grassroots levels. Men like Spalding caught the spirit of the age, and the business of baseball flourished, while the amateur game mostly languished
and is today preserved largely through the support of
schools and colleges.

Although they had a good rapport, Spalding and Alcock
were quite different sorts of men. Alcock was nothing if
not a good sport and was the pitcher in his first (and possibly last) game of baseball. Alcock's team won 17–5 after
only six innings, giving him a lifetime winning percentage
of 1.000 with an earned run average of 7.50. Unlike Spalding, who was a great player in his time, Alcock made up for
a lack of athletic talent with his enthusiasm for sport and
his skills as an administrator. In the snobbish and class-di-
vided world of Victorian Britain, he didn't quite fit in. His
family was wealthy but recently had risen from humble
origins, while he showed little interest in or aptitude for
the family shipping business. The aristocrats who played
cricket were happy for him to run the business side of the
game, but he was not quite one of them. The businessmen

who organized soccer teams were more like Spalding in outlook, and Alcock's family money created a distance between him and the ordinary players of the game.

In 1885 a crisis almost identical to that of baseball's threatened to split the amateur and professional game of association football (that is, soccer). Commercially oriented teams wanted to pay players so they could win championships, but the gentlemen and aristocrats wanted nothing to do with pay for play. Alcock was appointed by the Football Association to find a solution, and he put together a compromise that left both amateurs and professionals thinking they had won, while both agreed to accept the jurisdiction of the FA. The global governance of soccer today, whereby the revenues from professional competition subsidize the development of the game at the amateur level, is a direct consequence of this compromise.

Sporting competition seems to be a universal characteristic of human societies. Play, as a form of preparation for "real life," is in fact known to many more species than merely human beings, and is clearly a valuable step in the development of adolescents. A predisposition to enjoy play is advantageous because it promotes a more rapid development to maturity, and this advantage no doubt explains its prevalence in the animal world. But play is for children, play is informal, play is unstructured, play is only for fun. Adults show how seriously play is to be treated when they organize it into "sport." The meaning of the word *sport* is much debated, but one thing is obvious: the meaning of sport to different peoples in different times depends on the purpose that sport serves.

Sports, in a sense that we readily recognize today, were played in all the great ancient civilizations—Sumerians, Egyptians, Chinese, and Incas all had their sports, including wrestling, running, chariot races, boat races, and ball games. The rules of these games are not well understood today, but their social functions can still be grasped from art and ancient texts. The ancient sports had two purposes that stand out—one is military and the other is religious. Most sports prepared young men for war, and therefore early sports were reserved almost exclusively for men. Sporting competition helped establish social standing, without resort to deadly conflict. Those who were stronger displayed their supremacy over the weaker, and hence their fitness for leadership. In ancient legends the heroes often prove themselves in sporting contexts. In Homer's *Iliad*, games are held at the funeral of Patroclus, and the principal leaders of the Greek army hold a chariot race, with a slave woman as first prize. Such examples draw a stark picture of the purpose of sports in ancient society.

Perhaps more difficult to understand for the modern mind is their religious function. However, if we see ancient sports as a way to establish social standing and responsibilities, we see why these events required the sanction of the religious caste. Sport symbolized war, and even if a sporting contest was only a dress rehearsal, it was useful to rehearse a victory. "With God on our side" is no doubt the most effective battle cry in history, and therefore it makes sense to involve the gods in the preparation of warriors. This is nowhere clearer than in the Inca ball game, which bears similarities to both basketball and soccer. According to descriptions left by Spanish conquistadors, the winners had the right to ask for any possession belonging to the spectators, while the losers were sacrificed to the gods.

The most enduring tradition of the ancient sports is the Olympic Games, founded by the Greeks in 776 BCE.

The ancient Olympics involved 200-meter and 400-meter sprints, the pentathlon, long jump, discus and javelin throwing, forms of athletic competition that have more immediacy for us than any other ancient sports. Ancient Greece was a patchwork of independent city-states and overseas colonies, frequently at war with each other. Each city would organize their own games, but festivals such as the Olympics were "Panhellenic"—open to all Greeks. Games were held in honor of specific gods (the Olympics for Zeus, the Pythian Games for Apollo, the Isthmian Games for Poseidon), and the sanctity of the Olympics was indicated by the requirement that all military engagements cease during the games so that soldiers could attend. Here also, the games played a role in identifying military prowess, but the records of individual achievement and the stories associated with athletes give the games a modern feel. Great athletes came to be seen on a par with the heroes of myth. At first songs were written in their honor, soon statues were erected, and before long came the ticker-tape parade. Exaenetus of Agrigentum, winner of the Olympic footrace in 412 BCE, was driven through the streets of the city in a four-horse chariot followed by the city's three hundred most prominent citizens.

Twenty-five hundred years later, Greek sporting excesses have a thoroughly modern ring. Professional athletes traveled the circuit in pursuit of prizes paid for by the city they would represent (forget laurel wreaths, money and payments in kind were the norm), cities would bribe top athletes to switch allegiance, and athletes would bribe their rivals to lose (the route into the Olympic stadium was lined with statues paid for by athletes found guilty of cheating). Professional athletes became a race apart from the ordinary citizen who would only watch the games. There are stories of sexual excesses involving athletes in their postvictory celebrations. However, the identification of the success of the athlete with the status and well-being of the city is the most strikingly modern trait.

Roman games borrowed from the Greeks and other conquered nations, but also embodied "Roman virtues." The Romans developed spectator sport as a leisure activity to a degree that is breathtakingly modern—the Roman Coliseum, built in AD 72, could hold over fifty thousand spectators. The spectacles staged at the Coliseum involving fighting of one sort or another—gladiatorial contests, mock battles, and animal hunts. Strip away the fact that some of the contestants died, and you have a show that has much in common with professional wrestling today. Religious connections ceased to play a significant role, and the fights no longer had much to do with preparing citizens for a military career.

Gladiatorial contests were typically paid for by the wealthier citizens, and not least the emperor himself, as a way of buying public support. They were hugely expensive events and highly organized. Gladiators, as slaves, were traded in the market at prices that resemble those of a top baseball or soccer star today, and inscriptions survive bemoaning the inflation in prices for the top performers. Roman chariot racing also had a modern flavor; races in the Circus Maximus involved competition between four professional stables, each team sporting its own colors and attracting support from among all classes of society, from the emperor down. The drivers were the unquestioned superstars of the age, paid huge sums of money, frequently acting as if they were above the law, and mourned as heroes when they died. In one case, a distraught fan actually threw himself on the funeral pyre of a dead driver. In the later empire retired drivers sometimes pursued successful political careers.

Modernity in sport, it has been argued, consists of several elements—secularism, equality, bureaucratization, specialization, rationalization, quantification, and the obsession with records. But when we examine the ancient Roman chariot races, all of these elements seem present. And if this is true of an ancient civilization for which we have significant documentary records, who is to say that similar structures did not exist in ancient China or Mesoamerica, where the records are much sparser?

The Romans, of course, did not have stopwatches. A gulf separates the ancient world from our own. Almost all of the sports that we would call modern have been formalized over the last 250 years—soccer, football, baseball, golf, tennis, basketball, cricket, hockey, and modern track and field. Moreover, the formalization of these sports occurred almost entirely in one of two countries—Great Britain and the United States. The rules of the modern game of soccer derive from the rules of the Football Association (FA) created by eleven football (soccer) clubs in London in 1863, while the rules of baseball derive from the rules of the Knickerbocker Club of New York, written by Alexander Cartwright in 1845. Lawn tennis was invented and patented in England by Major Walter Wingfield in 1874, and basketball was invented in Springfield, Massachusetts, by James Naismith in 1891. The British in particular seemed to have been obsessed with the writing of rules and the creation of associations. For example, while both archery and boxing have been practiced since time immemorial throughout the world, the oldest known rules and associations for these sports came from Britain (the rules of boxing were written and published in London in 1743, and the Royal Toxophilite Society for the promotion of archery was founded in 1790, also in London).

Competition today is dominated by a select group of the sports that were formalized between 1750 and 1900. In particular, the modern obsession with sport focuses primarily on team sports—soccer, football, baseball, basketball, and cricket (beloved of one billion Indians). These sports, combined with the individual sports of tennis, golf, motor racing, and cycling, probably account for more than 80 percent of sports journalism around the world. All of these games had their first known rules and associations created in either Britain or the United States. Why should this be? Sociologists have advanced a number of theories, which tend to revolve around either industrialization or imperialism.

The industrialization theory argues that the rationalization of sport through rules and its organization into competitive units reflected the restructuring of Victorian society around industrial production in cities following the Industrial Revolution, which first flowered in Britain at the beginning of the nineteenth century and spread to the United States soon after. According to this view, regimentation of sport followed regimentation of work. The application of time-keeping, written records, mass production, and transportation all brought benefits to the organization of sport as much as it did to trade and commerce.

The imperialist theory argues that British sporting practice spread through the British Empire, on which the sun never set (at least in the nineteenth century). This happened not so much by forcing anyone to play British sports (indeed, the British frequently refused to play sport with their supposed inferiors) but through imitation. Along with military and economic power, accordingly, came dominance of culture and through influence British sporting practice spread. When the British Empire was supplanted by American economic power in the twentieth century, America's sporting practices also started to spread. The imperialist theory therefore focuses primarily on the means of diffusion rather than the origin of sports; implicitly, had another nation such as France or Germany been the dominant power in this era, it would have been their sporting practices that would have spread, rather than the British and American ones.

Both of these theories miss out on some interesting and important historical facts about the development of sport. They are essentially theories of the nineteenth century, when the most important steps in the development of modern sport may have taken place in the eighteenth century. Four modern sports, golf, cricket, horseracing, and boxing, set up rules and organizational structures in the mid-eighteenth century—before industrialization started, before Britain became the dominant power, before the United States was even born. Moreover, the two theories I've mentioned are silent on the institution that did most to create the revolution in sport, namely, the club.

Clubs are fundamental units of modern sport. The concept of an association or a federation is a modern one precisely because, as far as we know, the ancients did not have clubs in the sense that emerged in Europe in the eighteenth century. Indeed, historians and sociologists in recent years have recognized that one of the most fundamental transformations in Europe that led to the modern world was the development of associative activity—the formation of private clubs, where groups of individuals met to share pastimes without the interference of the state. In the ancient world, sporting spectacles were controlled entirely by the state, either as public religious festivals or expressions of largesse on the part of rulers (bread and circuses). In medieval Europe, sport meant either hunting or jousting or other forms of militaristic pastimes undertaken by the ruling class—a private affair for the privileged. The state offered little in the way of public entertainment and severely restricted the ability of individuals to congregate. Public assembly without the permission of the ruler or state could mean only one thing: rebellion. Kings and princes licensed certain forms of association, such as the guilds that monopolized trade, but these privileges carried obligations, usually in the form of taxes.

In this respect, English monarchs were like all other European rulers. This changed with Parliament's challenge to the authority of the king, which led to the Civil War of the 1640s and the beheading of King Charles in 1649. In a world where the monarch represented all aspects of the government and the state, this act changed forever the relationship between government and the people. The English republic was short lived, but when the monarchy was restored in 1660 it was under a vastly altered political dispensation. No longer did the government presume the right to regulate every aspect of private citizens' lives. No longer did the government see itself as the instigator of every public act or supervisor of every public affair. In short, the government withdrew from the total regulation of the public sphere, creating a gap into which a new public actor entered, the members' club. Perhaps the first such club in England was the Royal Society, an association of the leading scientists of the day, including Isaac Newton, Christopher Wren, and Robert Boyle. As a club, they met regularly to discuss the latest scientific ideas, and while the "Royal" label signaled government support, it did not mean that they required government sanction for anything they chose to do.

Less august clubs soon flourished in the developing coffeehouse societies of London, where traders and lawyers might meet to do business, and journalists might meet to discuss the latest tittle-tattle. Journalism itself was a consequence of the withdrawal of the state, the abolition of censorship in 1695 creating an essentially free press. Freedom of the press went hand in hand with formation of clubs, since people needed to know where to find like-minded individuals with whom they could associate. In the early years of the eighteenth century there was an astonishing explosion of clubs in England and Scotland, catering to every kind of pursuit, from science to the arts, to innocent pleasures such as music and the study of history, to serious moral reform and religious revival, and more profanely, to eating, drinking, and most of the remaining deadly sins. None of these activities were new, but their organization within the framework of a club certainly was.

Thus clubs also emerged for the pursuit of pastimes such as horseracing, cricket, and golf. Such activities had been around for hundreds of years, but in the early eighteenth century clubs were starting to be organized to pursue these sports on a regular basis. Like other clubs, sporting clubs were established as much for the opportunity to mix socially with like-minded people as to play the game itself—a function that golf, probably more than any other sport, fulfills even today. The clubhouse after a round of golf has always been the perfect place to meet friends and do business. The game itself, as a kind of duel between two players, might easily be seen as an evolution from medieval contests of strength and skill such as jousting. The prototypical team game was cricket.

Cricket, a bat-and-ball game involving two teams of eleven players, evolved at the beginning of the eighteenth century out of a village sport commonly played in the countryside around London. It became a tradition for the local gentry to participate, playing alongside their tenants and servants. Although social conservatives lamented the breakdown of class distinctions, there was typically a strict demarcation of the permitted roles of the players, and the yeoman farmer had to take care to keep his place. Yeomen "bowled"—that is, undertook the exhausting task of hurling the ball at the batsmen; gentlemen batted. As the game became fashionable among the dukes and earls of the royal court, it also became a vehicle for gambling—by the 1740s vast sums were being wagered on the outcome of a single game. Cricket became a small industry, with fields in London attracting large crowds to watch the nobility play, as well as drink beer and eat. The first club whose records survive, the Hambledon Club of Hampshire, kept a detailed history of games, wagers, and costs of food and drink consumed after the game. The Hambledon Club was founded around 1750 but was mainly active during the 1770s and 1780s, and was the arbiter of rules whenever disputes arose between teams. But Lord's Cricket Club in London (founded 1787), closer to noble patronage, soon displaced Hambledon, and from the 1790s was the ultimate authority on the rules of cricket. This step is crucial in the formation of modern sports— the idea that the exponents of a sport can establish their own government, independent of the state, functioning as a mini-state in its own right, with its own assembly, laws, executive powers, procedures for the settlement of disputes, and the power to tax and impose penalties. In cricket, this function was fulfilled by the Marylebone Cricket Club based at Lord's; in golf, it was the Royal and Ancient Golf Club (1754) in Edinburgh; in horseracing, it was the aristocratic Jockey Club (1752). To be sure, in their early days these organizations exercised only limited powers, but they formed the basis of organizations such as the International Olympic Committee (IOC) and the Fédération Internationale de Football Association (FIFA), which wield enormous power and prestige in the world today.

In English law, clubs and associations have no particular status. Anyone can form a club, for any legal purpose, without needing to obey any special rules. Unlike limited corporations, the law does not recognize a club as a legal person, and a member of a club that owes debts will soon discover that a club liability is in fact a personal liability. The absence of any legal status reflects the independence of such organizations from the control of the state. The fact that English law never interfered in the formation of associations by private citizens indicates how much freedom was left to individual initiative. By the end of the eighteenth century visitors to England became quite bored with the tendency of the English to proclaim their liberties and to declare that other nations lived in servitude. Contemporary Germans and Frenchmen often found this national pride quite puzzling, because they did not see what the English were free to do that they were not. But freedom of association did mean something. It was certainly not permitted elsewhere in Europe. In France any association required a license from the king, while in Germany and Austria absolutist rulers tended to interfere in every aspect of private life. In revolutionary America, by contrast, the colonists sought independence in order to preserve their English liberties, not least the freedom of association guaranteed by the First Amendment.

The development of modern sports is a curious by-product of these politics. In nineteenth-century England there was an explosion of sporting organizations. Private schools such as Eton, Rugby, and Harrow played an important role, mostly through the initiative of the boys themselves, who not only played the established game of cricket in the summer, but led the development of football games. Having played these games at school and university, they formed clubs in the towns and cities and were soon being emulated by enthusiasts from all levels of society—there was nothing to stop workingmen from forming a cricket or football club. Similarly in the United States, private associations, notably the Knickerbocker Club of New York, led the formation of modern baseball, while university students from Harvard, Princeton, and Yale created American football and a social worker from the YMCA created basketball. The fountainhead of this creativity was the plethora of clubs created by Americans, largely in pursuit of their leisure.

France and Germany, by contrast, made only limited contributions to the development of modern sport. In France, the absolutism of the monarch was followed by the Napoleonic legal code, which included a law that no private association of more than twenty members could be formed without formal permission from the state. The purpose of this law was to suppress the potential for revolutionary agitation—the effect was to suppress initiative. Even for a sport such as cycling, in which the French produced more innovations and showed more interest than almost any other, the first clubs were created in England. By the latter half of the nineteenth century clubs such as the Racing Club and Stade Française finally established themselves, but by this time the British and Americans had already produced a menagerie of sporting associations. In Baron Pierre de Coubertin, the man who revived the Olympic Games, France produced one of the greatest administrators in the history of sport. But throughout his career he looked primarily to English models and advocated English sporting ideals. When the law prohibiting private associations was finally repealed in 1901, there was an explosion of sporting activity in France, but apart from cycling the sports they adopted were largely those created in England, notably rugby football and association football (soccer).

The evolution of modern sports in Germany is also strikingly influenced by politics. The father of modern sport in Germany was Friedrich Ludwig Jahn, a German nationalist who witnessed the defeat of the Prussian army by Napoleon at the battle of Jena in 1806 and attributed it to the lack of fitness of the Germans. To rectify this weakness he founded the Turnen movement, a gymnastic association that spawned clubs all over the German states. These clubs associated gymnastic fitness with preparation for war and the unification of Germany into a single state. Jahn introduced new gymnastic exercises such as the parallel bars and horse, but his intentions were as much political as sporting. Following the defeat of Napoleon, the Turnen movement was suppressed by the Austrian chancellor Metternich, who feared that it might challenge the supremacy of the Austrian emperor. With no freedom of association, Germans had no right to form clubs of any kind. In 1848 a wave of revolutionary activity spread across Europe, and in Germany a national convention was established to create a liberal political regime. The aged Jahn was feted as progenitor of the revolutionary movement, and his clubs were revived all over the German lands. The revolution, however, failed, and many of the Turnen movement activists went into exile to the United States. In the latter half of the nineteenth century Turnen clubs were established all across America, and Abraham Lincoln's bodyguard was made up of German gymnasts. The Turnen movement also attracted some interest in France, and gymnastics was largely promoted by the state as a means for ensuring military readiness. Such motives differed significantly from those of an anglophile such as de Coubertin.

Sporting clubs finally achieved political legitimacy in the 1860s as Germany moved toward unification, but they always retained their strong political flavor. There developed a socialist sporting movement aimed at creating political consciousness through sport, while the state attempted to suppress such activities. During the Nazi period all sporting activities were absorbed into the Nazi Party itself—for the purposes of molding the master race. In the postwar era sporting clubs developed into a kind of social service, funded by the state and provided for all citizens, offering the possibility for participation in all sports. Every community in Germany has its state-funded *Turnverein*, and these associations are the most important providers of sports for children. Similarly in France the concern of the state to ensure that its adult males were ready for military action has evolved into state provision of sporting facilities for all throughout the country.

By now it should be apparent that the development of modern sports went hand in hand with social and political ideals and objectives. For the English, the sports whose rules they laid down were deemed to represent above all the nature of the English character. In 1851, the Reverend James Pycroft, writing the first history of the game, declared, "The game of Cricket, philosophically considered, is a standing panegyric on the English character: none but an orderly and sensible race would so amuse themselves." This fact, along with the tedium that most foreigners associate with the game, helps to explain why it did not spread to most countries. While cricket clubs were established across Europe in the nineteenth century, and while it was the most popular game in the United States until the end of the 1850s (the first ever international cricket match was played between the United States and Canada in 1840), most non-English people balked at playing a game that was so identified with being British. Except, of course, for the colonies of the British Empire. Here cricket thrived, either because colonists aspired to prove their ties to the mother country, or because indigenous peoples wanted to prove themselves against their colonial masters. To this day cricket thrives in the former empire—Australia, India, Pakistan, South Africa, Sri Lanka, New Zealand, and islands of the Caribbean that were under British rule play and watch the game enthusiastically.

Baseball also experienced mixed fortunes in its attempts to spread itself around the globe. We have already met Al Spalding, one of the first professional baseball players, later manager and general sports impresario. To spread the game, he undertook two international tours, one to Britain in 1874 and a celebrated tour around the globe in 1888. Another global tour was organized in 1911. Spalding wanted to persuade the British to take up the game, but they were never likely to forsake cricket. He had a little success in Australia, none in Europe, but he ignored the biggest adopter of the game abroad. Japan looked abroad to acquire modern skills following the forced opening of the country by Commodore Perry. Shipbuilding was copied from the British, the army from the Germans, the education system from the French, and physical education from the Americans. Baseball was introduced by Horace Wilson, a missionary working at the University of Tokyo, during the 1870s and became firmly established as a national sport when a Japanese college team defeated the Yokohama Athletic Club, made up of expatriate Americans, in 1896. Baseball also spread into those parts of the Caribbean that were under American influence, most notably Cuba, where the game was played from the 1860s onwards.

The sport that has been most successful at spreading around the world is soccer. It is more adaptable than most, playable with almost no equipment and in almost any weather, in contrast to cricket and baseball, which require both equipment and dry conditions. Soccer also benefited from being seen as not too closely tied to the country from which it originated. While the foundation of the Football Association in London in 1863 established the rules by which the game is played more or less unchanged to the present day, most cultures have a tradition of kicking balls, and there are many claims of priority (the Chinese, for instance, can identify their own version of football played more than two thousand years ago, while the Italians rechristened the game *calcio* after the Florentine ball game played in the sixteenth century). During the late nineteenth century, when Britain dominated international trade and commerce, and British citizens were present in all corners of the globe, doing business and playing their sports in their leisure time, local bystanders quickly took up soccer as a game that they could play in their own way and adapt to their own style. Often children of the European elites who had been educated in England took back a soccer ball to their own country and started a club (such was the case, for instance, in Switzerland and Portugal). In other countries local players took over clubs founded by the English (these clubs often retain their original English names, for example, the Grasshoppers of Zurich, AC Milan, and Athletic de Bilbao—rather than the Spanish *Atlético*). In South America, which had very close commercial ties with Britain, soccer rapidly spread among the elites of Argentina, Uruguay, and Brazil. Moreover, once the game became established, English teams were regularly invited to tour—not only in Europe but also to Buenos Aires and Rio de Janeiro. Again, the names of South American teams such as the Corinthians and Newell's Old Boys betray their British influence.

Notwithstanding these influences, each country developed its own style of play and in this way made the game their own, perhaps most gloriously demonstrated by the world-beating teams produced by Brazil. The fact that soccer could be molded to local styles and customs gave it a universal appeal that would have been impossible for a sport as English as cricket or as American as baseball. Enough countries played the sport by 1904 for the creation of an international association (FIFA) to organize games and maintain a common set of rules. The British were unenthusiastic about FIFA, and hence much of the early development of the organization took place without British influence, furthering the sense of a truly international game.

If clubs are the basic unit of modern sports, the relationship between competing clubs defines the organizational structure of any sport and its commercial possibilities. Modern sports were not created with business in mind—they were invented as a way for men, usually well-to-do men, to socialize. Sporting contests were essentially an excuse for conviviality. However, these contests soon attracted spectators, and once spectators were present, the opportunity to do business arose. In the eighteenth century, commercial opportunities were created by the desire of participants and spectators to gamble on the outcome of a game. As cricket matches started to draw fashionable crowds, opportunities to sell food, drink, and other necessaries also emerged, and before long entrepreneurs went the whole hog and staged games, paid the players, and charged for entry.

Religion, formally or informally, goes hand in hand with sport; for this reason commercialism in sport has always been considered profane, and throughout modern history there have been attempts to suppress the association of sports with commercialism. Early modern sports in Britain and America were created largely as a leisure activity for the upwardly mobile. Having already acquired a fortune, such people tended to frown on commercial activities. They preferred to think they were motivated by the challenge and by the social aspect of sport. Engaging in sport was the ultimate statement about freedom—including freedom from commercial constraints—hence the desire to keep money out of sport. This creed reached its apotheosis in Victorian England, where the pursuit of money came to be seen as the ultimate sin. However, similar attitudes were to be found among the members of the Knickerbocker Club in New York. When promoters started to see an opportunity for making a buck by organizing professional baseball, the gentlemen of the fashionable New York clubs recoiled in horror. Amateurs and professionals went their own ways, and as it turned out professional baseball was a great success.

The progenitor of all modern sports leagues was the National League of baseball created by William Hulbert in 1876. Freed from the interference of the amateur gentlemen, Hulbert created a business model that essentially survives today in the American major leagues. The model relies on cooperation between independent franchises, each of which is granted a local monopoly, an incentive to promote the game in the locality. Franchise owners agree collectively on policies that promote league interests so long as they also promote the franchise's interests—these policies revolve around ways to hold down players' wages and limit competition for the acquisition of new talent. Operating as a closed system, the league forces each team to recognize its dependence on the commercial well-being of the other teams. The National League brought credibility to baseball at a time when it was in danger of losing popularity because of gambling, match fixing, and frequent cancellation of games. By creating a stable business enterprise, in which every team owner possessed a significant stake, Hulbert invented a sporting organization that became synonymous with the American way of life and survives today in the form of Major League Baseball. Hulbert's ideas and principles were largely copied by other successful sports leagues such as the National Football League (NFL) and the National Basketball Association (NBA).

Outside of the American major leagues, the business model of sport was designed largely to minimize profit

MARK & HELEN OSTERLIN LIBRARY
NORTHWESTERN MICHIGAN COLLEGE
TRAVERSE CITY, MICHIGAN 49686-3061

opportunities and to keep sport free of commercial motives. This is clearly demonstrated in the modern Olympic Games, which until 1980 barred professional athletes from competing. The Olympic ideal, as viewed by Baron de Coubertin, relied on athletes motivated purely by glory. Sport, properly understood, existed on a higher plane than mere commerce. De Coubertin was enormously influenced by what he understood to be the British model of sport. In Britain, the development of modern sports was largely led by aristocrats and the emerging middle class. Membership in a sporting club was a status symbol—much like belonging to a prestigious golf club today—and one way to maintain status was to exclude poorer members of society by requiring membership fees and even by scheduling games at times when working people would not be able to attend. The ultimate symbol of respectability in Victorian Britain was to be a man of leisure and to have no need to work. In cricket this snobbery manifested itself by dividing participants into "gentlemen"—those who played for the love of the game, and "players"—those who required a wage to be able to play. Professionals were needed since gentlemen in general liked only to bat. In soccer, however, the gentlemen amateurs saw no need to mix with professionals at all, and in the original rules of the Football Association only amateurs were allowed to play.

As soccer's popularity spread, however, entrepreneurs saw the chance to make money by hiring the best players and charging spectators to watch, much in the way the professional teams had emerged in baseball. The same conflict between amateurs and professionals arose, but the soccer authorities ended up taking a very different route, thanks to the diplomacy of Charles Alcock. Rather than

going their separate ways, as in baseball, the amateurs
agreed to a compromise with the professionals—their
right to play the game was recognized as long as the rules
of conduct remained under the control of the Football
Association (FA), set up in 1863 to promote the game, and
in those days dominated by amateurs.

The practical consequence of this compromise was that
the soccer world has been governed ever since by national
and international committees that legislate every aspect
of the game, including the professional game. These governments have the power to tax the professional leagues
in order to subsidize the development of the game elsewhere, something that has been an important factor in
the spread of soccer. The governing bodies have also req-
uisitioned the employees of the professional clubs on a
regular basis to participate in international tournaments
such as the World Cup.

But the gentlemen amateurs also imposed regulations
on the operation of professional soccer clubs that restricted their capacity to make money. Just as in America,
entrepreneurs recognized the opportunity to make money
once soccer became popular, but in England the FA imposed rules that prevented owners from paying themselves large dividends out of company profits, and even
forbade the directors of soccer clubs from paying themselves a salary. Professional soccer in this way became essentially a "not-for-profit" activity, with all profits being
plowed back into the purchase of players to improve the
performance of the team. Moreover, with profit virtually
excluded as a motive for owning a soccer club, the game
attracted wealthy individuals who saw ownership as a way
to build their reputation in the local community by investing in the club's success. The virtual absence of the

profit motive had another significant effect, on the rules of competition. The first professional soccer league, the Football League, was founded in 1888, influenced to a significant degree by the precedent of baseball's National League. However, the Football League wanted to embrace as many teams as possible. Instead of limiting membership to a fixed number of franchises, the league developed a system to permit all eligible professional clubs to participate and have a chance to rise to the top: the promotion and relegation system. As the number of teams wanting to participate in the Football League expanded, it created new divisions, and adopted the rule that at the end of each season the worst-performing teams would be sent down a division (relegation) and be replaced by the best-performing teams from below. In this way, every professional team, however lowly, knows that one day it might compete at the highest level, while even the mightiest champion knows that one day it might fall into a lower division. These rules have implications for the commercial operation of clubs.

Through FIFA, the organizational system of English soccer spread to Europe and the rest of the world. Outside of the United States, soccer is almost everywhere organized along the lines originally developed in England. Moreover, these organizational principles have spread to other sports. For example, the system of league organization in European basketball bears a closer resemblance to the soccer model than it does to the structure of basketball in the United States. Even in the United States, commercial motives are restrained to a significant degree in college sports. Varsity sports in the United States can trace their roots back to the games played in British schools and universities, and the same principles of amateurism have been retained by the National Collegiate Athletic Association (NCAA).

In recent decades the amateur model has come under increasing pressure. The advent of television created huge audiences and immensely valuable broadcast rights across all the major sports. Within the framework of professional for-profit sport, these pressures have been assimilated in ways typical of any business—through adaptation to the needs of the broadcasters and through competition to provide a spectacle that is as attractive as possible to those who pay to watch. Competition has also fueled increasing rewards for those who play at the highest level. For sports influenced significantly by the principles of amateurism, however, the compromises have been uneasy. Only in the 1980s did the Olympic movement start to relax its rules against professionalism. Over the years the Olympics have become a lucrative business, undermining the image of the games as a festival of fellowship and goodwill. The NCAA in the United States has maintained its ban on payment to players while generating billions of dollars in broadcast revenue, leading to conduct on the part of colleges and coaches that often seems unfair and even corrupt. Even in professional sports like soccer, the organizational structures created in the spirit of open competition have come under pressure. In a world where relegation from a top division can cost tens of millions of dollars, the competition to avoid the drop—both legal and illegal—threatens to undermine the health of the sport. As new generations of owners and managers enter the field, attracted by the commercial possibilities of popular sports, there is pressure for reform in the direction of a more commercial outlook. In many cases these pressures have given rise to a heated debate over the "soul" of sport, and its proper place in the modern world.

Modern sports are an essential feature of modern societies. This chapter has outlined how these modern sports emerged out of civil societies characterized by freedom of association. This background gave rise to an organizational model involving the alliance of independent clubs within national and international federations, built largely on amateur, not-for-profit principles. Two important variants have emerged alongside this model. First, in many countries, especially where freedom of association has been limited, the state has taken a leading role in organizing and funding sport, often with specific goals in mind such as military preparedness or entertainment for the masses. Second, a purely commercially oriented form of professional sport, such as Major League Baseball, emerged in the United States and has spread to some other countries. Each of these variants has been influenced by broadcast technologies, to the point where the viability of traditional models is increasingly coming under question.

Two

ORGANIZING COMPETITION

Freakonomics, the best-seller that uses economics to explain behavior most people wouldn't think has anything to do with economics, called Japanese sumo wrestling corrupt. "Cheating to lose is sport's premier sin," declared authors Steven Levitt and Stephen Dubner. They showed that bouts that are more critical to one wrestler than to his opponent tend to be won by the one who needs it most. In the next bout, the winner then "repays" his opponent, who wins the follow-up match far more often than he would under normal circumstances.

But is that cheating? Whether you think so or not depends on the culture you come from. In the intensively competitive world of the University of Chicago economics department (from which Levitt hails), failing to give your all in a competition is a sin. However, in many other cultures, it is simply good manners. Consider an FA Cup soccer game between Arsenal and Sheffield United a few years ago. After seventy-five minutes the game was at 1–1, when an Arsenal player was injured. A Sheffield player, following the unwritten code of fair play, kicked the ball out of bounds so that the game could stop and the injured player receive treatment. At the restart, an Arsenal player, also following the code, threw the ball toward a Sheffield player, restoring the state of affairs at the point of the injury. However, the Arsenal striker Kanu, playing his first game for Arsenal (indeed his first game in England), did not realize what was intended, and pounced on the ball. His pass then led to an Arsenal goal that decided the match.

So distressed was Arsenal's manager by this failure of soccer etiquette that he offered to play the match again. The offer was accepted by Sheffield and sanctioned by the governing body, and so the game was indeed replayed a few days later. Not "cheating to lose" perhaps, but certainly not an example of "win at all costs" (in fact, Arsenal won the replay 1–0, but this time there was no argument). It may be a cliché, but there is more to sport than winning, and even Vince Lombardi, the football coach who notoriously asserted that "winning is the only thing," later in life admitted to regretting this extreme statement.

Of course, when sport is played for pleasure, competitors often care about more than just winning. In commercial sports the players and the teams are supplying a form of public entertainment, and successful sports organizations have learned to supply what fans and consumers want. In this chapter we consider how organizers design contests that will appeal to fans.

The modern business of sport emerged because large numbers of consumers were willing to pay for the privilege of following sporting contests. Even before radio and television expanded the potential audience beyond the physical limits of the stadium, a sporting press had emerged to provide fans with information about forthcoming games and analysis of games already played. How did humanity become so obsessed with sporting contests? More importantly for those who want to profit from the organization of sporting contests, what is it that makes people interested in following a particular sport? Historians, sociologists, and psychologists have written on the subject, and each provides us with some clues. From history we learn that sport is a matter of culture, most of us following the sport that we grew up following. This is why Americans have been so slow to take up the global version of football, and why Europeans have proved so resistant to the American version, or to baseball for that matter. However, some sports do have truly global appeal—motor racing and tennis being two examples. Sociologists have pointed to the tribalism associated with following sport, and the way it gets bound up in the sense of personal identity. This tribalism can erupt into violence when fans of one team develop a passionate hatred of supporters of a rival team. Psychologists have emphasized ways in which sporting contests arouse our emotions, creating intense personal experiences, a kind of high hard to find in the rest of our lives. Spectators project their own personality into the contest, participating vicariously in a heroic struggle.

Demand, therefore, can be boiled down to some key factors. First, there is the quality of the contest, which is a function of the skills of the contestants, but also of the effort they devote to winning. Second, there is the outcome. One might think that a tense outcome is more exciting than a predictable one and that evenly balanced contests are desirable. However, there is good evidence that fans prefer a high probability that the home team will win, that is, an unbalanced contest. Of course, fans also care about prices, what they have to pay to watch the game at the stadium or on TV (watching commercials on free-to-air TV is a kind of payment). Finally, there is the total experience, such as the quality of the stadium and the importance of the game from a social perspective.

The contest organizer, therefore, needs to consider how a contest can be designed to create the most intense competition between opponents. This chapter explores the problem of economic design.

The Winner-Take-All Contest

Let's begin by thinking about a simple setup in order to see how the economics of a contest works. Imagine the problem faced by the organizer of a footrace. Suppose that the organizer has already arranged a venue and plans to sell tickets to watch the race in order to generate the maximum profit possible.

The organizer has two main issues to consider—how to attract entrants and how to make the race interesting for spectators. The time-honored way to achieve both of these objectives is to offer a prize to the winner only: the winner-take-all contest. An economic model of this arrangement was first analyzed by Gordon Tullock in the 1960s. In his model, each contestant has a probability of winning the prize that depends on his or her contribution to the total effort—the bigger the share of the total effort exerted, the higher the probability of winning the prize. If we assume that every contestant is of equal ability, the mathematics turns out to be relatively simple. Each contestant is assumed to maximize his or her expected return from participating in the contest, which is equal to the probability of winning the prize multiplied by the value of the prize, minus the effort expended in trying to win.

The choice of effort level is dictated by the usual economic calculation of "marginal benefits" and "marginal costs." According to this equation, effort increases to the point where the marginal gain (meaning the extra benefit expected by the contestant from supplying an extra unit of effort) equals the marginal cost of contributing effort. In this case, marginal gain equals the marginal increase in the probability of winning multiplied by the value of the prize. Note that this calculation depends on each contestant's beliefs about the effort the others will make. If contestants are mistaken in these beliefs—under- or overestimating rivals' effort—then they will experience regret, thinking they made too little or too much effort. Only when each contestant correctly predicts the effort of every other contestant will the result of the race be an equilibrium—a situation where all contestants do the best they should expect to do given the choices of everyone else. This concept was first explained by the Nobel Prize–winning mathematician John Nash. In fact, this is an example of a "Nash equilibrium," meaning that the choice of each contestant represents a "best response" to the choices of all the other contestants. The Nash equilibrium is the most reliable prediction of the outcome of the contest, since for any other outcome at least one contestant must regret the choice that he or she made. In other words, only at a Nash equilibrium can we say that no one is making a mistake.

The Nash equilibrium of this contest has some interesting properties. At the equilibrium, every contestant supplies the same amount of effort, since everyone responds to the incentive in the same way (this is a consequence of assuming contestants are identical). Reasonably enough, the effort level increases as the prize gets bigger, or the cost of supplying effort gets smaller (the cost of effort in a marathon is larger than the cost of effort in the 100-meter dash). The amount of effort supplied also depends on the "technology" of the contest.

Technology here means the way in which efforts are transformed into winning probabilities. Again, we suppose that each contestant's effort is weighted in the same way, so that if two contestants supply identical effort, they have the same probability of winning. The issue therefore is simply the effectiveness of effort. At one extreme, we could imagine that the contestant with the highest effort always wins—even if that effort is only slightly higher than any rival's effort. In this case we say the technology is perfectly discriminating, and the contest becomes an auction in which the prize goes to the highest "bidder" (an athlete's effort is equivalent to a bid in an auction). At the other extreme, effort might have no effect on the probability of winning (a pure lottery). More realistically, the way in which the contest is decided will lie somewhere between these two extremes. Sporting contests are usually designed to be highly discriminating, since the more discriminating the contest, the more effort the contestants will supply. Organizers interested in maximizing effort will want the technology to discriminate as effectively as possible between high and low effort.

Perhaps the most interesting result is that the effort level of each contestant decreases as the number of contestants increases. This may not seem obvious, but should be quite clear on reflection. The more contestants, the less likely that your individual effort will triumph, and therefore the lower the returns to making effort. When returns are low, effort itself will also be low. In this context, therefore, the best contest is one involving a small number of highly motivated contestants. That is why race organizers invite a small, elite field of runners when they want to stage a high-quality race. This result also has interesting implications for the decision about how large a league should be. In the United States, leagues have tended to expand in numbers over time in order to reach a larger audience, and sometimes to preempt the development of rival leagues. Little thought has been given to "optimal" league size, although in recent years Major League Baseball has also threatened to contract (between 1903 and 1961 there were sixteen major league teams, by 1998 the number had been expanded to thirty, and in 2001 the commissioner, Bud Selig, proposed that two franchises be axed). One problem with overexpansion is that owners may feel they have little chance of winning and so are unwilling to invest in the team.

In examining this type of contest, Tullock and his followers were interested in a specific question: how much profit (that is, the excess of benefits over costs) will contestants expect to make from the contest? Specifically, he drew an analogy with competition between firms in a market. Economists have long understood that monopolists can extract a profit (called an economic rent) from consumers by charging high prices, but that the introduction of competition erodes profit. As competition increases, prices are driven down to the point where, if there is enough competition, all economic rent will disappear—a state of affairs typically referred to as perfect competition. Would the same be true in contests? Certainly it is true in the model that the contestant's expected profit decreases as the number of contestants increases—but will the economic rent ever be completely dissipated?

The answer, it turns out, depends on what we assume about the winning technology. If the probability of winning is not too affected by effort, contestants expect to make a profit, and profits are always positive no matter how many contestants there are. Since these profits get smaller when more contestants enter, they almost vanish for a large enough contest.

However, if the winning probability is highly sensitive to effort (so that small differences in effort lead to large differences in prospects), then the contest becomes unstable. That is because the equilibrium effort keeps on increasing as the sensitivity of winning to effort increases, to the point where the total effort could exceed the value of the prize. The contestants are involved in a rat race. They know the prize is not worth the effort, but once they have entered the contest, giving up is worse. In these circumstances, why would anyone enter the contest? Well, if everyone else thinks the same way and decides not to enter, then someone can enter the race uncontested, which would clearly be profitable (uncontested elections are not uncommon in democracies when the cost of running for office is very high). Of course, an uncontested race is of little interest to spectators, and so contest organizers try to create enough randomness in a contest to ensure that effort alone cannot guarantee victory.

But if the outcome of a contest truly is highly sensitive to effort, the theory predicts that potential contestants will "randomize," meaning that rather than make a firm decision whether to enter the contest, they flip a coin. As a result, sometimes the contestant doesn't enter the contest (no profit, no loss), sometimes several contestants enter (the winner makes a profit, but the losses of the losers exceed the profit of the winner), and sometimes only one contestant enters (and wins the prize with no effort). Or maybe no one enters, and so the contest does not take place. Overall, these plans amount to an equilibrium because everyone has the expectation that they will at least break even, rather than being certain to make a loss. Of course, in some situations contestants take losses, but if contestants think about entering a series of contests, they can expect to break even over the long term.

Now, this may all sound a little far-fetched, and Tullock himself tried to argue that this randomizing outcome (or "mixed strategy equilibrium," as it is called in the literature) could not be the right answer. But in fact randomization is the solution to lots of practical problems. For example, consider penalty shots in soccer. A player usually prefers to aim at one side of the goal—left or right— depending on his or her abilities. However, even if a player is better at shooting to the left, say, it makes no sense *always* to shoot to the left. If the player always aims to the same side, the goalkeeper can predict where the ball will go and so have a great chance of saving the penalty. The player has to shoot right *sometimes*, creating uncertainty in the goalkeeper and so increasing the probability of scoring. Research by economists has shown that professional players are in fact extremely skilled at randomizing, that is, mixing up their shots. This does not mean that they have a detailed appreciation of economic theory, just that good players score goals, and the process of selection leads those with an instinctive appreciation of the best strategy to rise to the top.

However, what the contest theory tells us is that winner-take-all contests can be very high-risk activities involving substantial losses for the losers. If small differences in effort have big impacts on the result, contestants find themselves in an arms race, where they always feel that a bit more effort might tip things in their favor. Once you have entered such a contest, there is no limit to what you might do to win. Unless you have a large appetite for risk taking, it may be better not to enter such a contest.

While we may enjoy watching others participate in these contests, most of us prefer to participate in a winner-take-all contest only if chance plays a large enough role that no contestant thinks it worthwhile to get involved in an arms race. A good example is TV game shows, such as *Who Wants to Be a Millionaire?* In the United States would-be contestants call a toll-free number and answer a quiz in order to get onto the show, but in other countries they have to pay the cost of the telephone call, and thus the show makes money by sharing the call revenue with the telephone company. Suppose all potential contestants had to take a two-hour math test in order to qualify. Most people would not bother, knowing that their chance of success was small, and as a result, only math professors would appear on the show. To persuade people to call in, the questions are sufficiently random and easy to ensure that no one has a particular advantage, and so millions of people are tempted to call. For spectator sports, on the other hand, only the very best need apply.

Extensions

The winner-take-all contest gives us some essential insights into the fundamental problems of organizing a competition. However, it is a relatively simple problem, and real contests may differ in significant ways. A single prize, for the winner, may not be the ideal reward structure, and contestants don't all have the same ability. Moreover, a footrace, in which all contestants run simultaneously, is different from a tennis tournament or a basketball league. Even in a footrace there are complexities we haven't yet looked at: as the race progresses, athletes frequently reevaluate the effort they are prepared to devote to winning.

Alternative Reward Structures

Most contests that award gold medals also award silver and bronze medals. Sometimes prizes are also awarded for the absolute level of performance (time, score, and so on), not just for order of finish. If we assume that the person putting on the contest has a certain amount of money and wants to maximize effort, second and third prizes may not seem like a good idea. Reducing the reward for winning (which requires the most effort) in order to reward second place (which requires less effort) undermines the incentive to supply effort. To put it another way, second prizes are rewards for losing, and so they diminish the incentive to be a winner. This is true as long as all contestants are of equal ability. However, if they aren't equal, then we can see why second prizes make sense.

Suppose there are three contestants in a race—Donald Duck, Daffy Duck, and the Roadrunner. The Roadrunner is easily the fastest, and the contestants know it. If there is only a prize for first place, Donald and Daffy have little reason to compete, and they might as well not enter the race. But without Donald and Daffy, there is no race, and the Roadrunner can take a leisurely stroll. With the introduction of a second prize, the situation looks different. Even if Donald and Daffy have no hope of winning first place, they can compete for second and therefore have an incentive to make an effort. Note also that they now affect the behavior of the Roadrunner. Even if it takes little effort to beat Donald and Daffy, it is still more than was required when they didn't enter the race. Thus the introduction of a second prize increases the effort of all three contestants!

This result depends on the distribution of abilities. With the Roadrunner, Donald, and Daffy, a silver medal works wonders. But a second prize is not a good idea if two contestants are strong and one is weak. In that case, a second ribbon undermines the competition between the two strong contestants, who know they are going to win a prize without putting in much effort. So we conclude that the optimal prize structure depends on the distribution of abilities. The fact that in practice most races have a small number of high-ability athletes and a large number of lower-ability athletes helps explain why most races have multiple prizes.

So far we have assumed that prizes are the right kind of incentive—after all, that is what one normally expects as the reward for success in a contest. However, it is a good idea to step back for a moment and ask what is so good about a prize. In some ways, prizes in a contest are not a very good method to get effort from people, precisely because they make a person's reward depend on the actions of others. For example, if I want you to mow my lawn, I will usually pay you some fee, let us say $10, perhaps with a bonus if I'm really pleased with your work. Suppose instead I got together with nine other householders and offered you the opportunity to take part in a contest, where a prize of $100 would be paid to the fastest mower and no one else would get paid anything. How likely is it that you would find this an attractive deal? Contests introduce risk, and most of us prefer to avoid risk. You might agree to enter the contest if in addition to the prize for winning I paid you a guaranteed fee, but this would probably end up being more expensive for me than simply paying you a fixed fee. This illustrates why contest-style incentives are used sparingly in real life outside sports. Even in footraces, top athletes are typically paid an appearance fee—a fixed amount for doing the job, much like paying someone who mows my lawn—and few sports professionals survive on prize money alone. We will consider the issue of providing appropriate incentives for contestants in more detail in chapter 4. For the time being it is enough to say that prizes ensure high levels of effort once the contestants have been persuaded to enter in the first place.

Alternative Contest Structures

A footrace of the sort we have been imagining is easy to analyze because all contestants compete simultaneously and must come in first, second, third, and so on. However, few contests are like that. For example, the Olympic 100-meter sprint consists of several rounds, where the fastest runners in each round progress to the next. In this sort of contest, what is the ideal number of contestants in each round, and what is the ideal number of rounds? Too many rounds and the runners will tire or the championship will take too long. Too few rounds and the number of contestants has to be scaled down.

A tennis tournament, however, is a different kind of contest. Here contestants can compete in pairs, and therefore any contest with more than two players must have more than one round. There are two main variants for this type of contest, the round-robin and the knockout. In a round-robin, or league format, each contestant plays every other contestant and is awarded points for wins, and the player with the highest number of points at the end is the winner. As we observed in the previous chapter, the league format was invented for the conduct of professional baseball championships, and the world's oldest surviving league is baseball's National League, founded in 1876. A knockout, or elimination contest, is a much more venerable structure and was known in the ancient world. Here contestants are paired and the winner in each round progresses to the next. The principal subtlety in an elimination tournament is the way in which players are drawn against each other. Most important tournaments adopt a seeding procedure, whereby the strongest contestants are kept apart in the early rounds, with the intention of ensuring that only the best reach the final rounds of competition.

Elimination tournaments tend to produce upsets, while round-robins ensure that the overall winner is the player who performs best on average. Elimination tournaments tend to raise the effort levels in any given contest, since much more is at stake than in a league format. Elimination tournaments tend to be more prevalent in individual sports, such as tennis and golf, than in team sports, where league formats dominate. One possible reason for this may have to do with the motives of the organizers. A league format is a better option for the contestants: weak contestants play a guaranteed number of games rather than facing early elimination, while strong contestants are insured against the risk of a single poor performance. However, an elimination format is often more exciting for the spectators. Tournaments organized by an independent promoter tend to have an elimination format since the spectacle will be more exciting—tennis tournaments such as Wimbledon or the US Open are good examples. By contrast, when a tournament is organized by the contestants themselves, they tend to choose the safer league format.

The choice of format may also reflect the preferences of spectators in other ways. The preferences of a tennis fan are likely to differ from those of a football fan. In the former case the fan is likely to be interested in the game itself, and may be relatively indifferent to the identity of the players, as long as they are playing at the highest level. Thus tournament organizers have an incentive to attract the best players regardless of who they are. In team sports fans typically attach themselves to a particular club, usually one that is close to where they live, and hence the identity of the team matters. A league format provides more competition for fans in a given location, and therefore the organizers of team sports are likely to attract a bigger audience using a league format. In fact, we can find examples in history where league formats have superseded knockout structures. In England the first proper soccer tournament was the FA Cup, a knockout tournament started in 1872 and played to the present day. Once professional clubs became established, their owners became dissatisfied with the uncertainty of the FA Cup format and started the Football League in 1888. While both competitions survive, the league has been more successful in attracting fans and developing clubs.

Yet sports league organizers have always recognized the value of the championship race in maintaining fans' interest, and have taken steps to ensure that the outcome is not settled too quickly. Perhaps by accident, the recognition by baseball's National League of the American League as its equal created the first great play-off competition, the World Series in 1903. Following this example, the other major leagues in the United States have created play-offs for the championship, and in more recent decades adopted a system of play-offs that meant that at the end of the regular season many teams can still win the championship. But if too many teams reach the play-offs, the value of performance in the regular season can be undermined. In the 2000–2001 season of the league championship organized by the English Rugby Union eight of twelve teams advanced to the play-offs!

Strategy and Races

The Tour de France takes place over twenty-one stages, and the winner is the cyclist with the lowest cumulative time over the entire course. Winning an individual stage, therefore, is not essential. Indeed, it would be possible never to win a stage but win the entire race. Strategy in the Tour de France is notoriously complex. The lead racers have large teams to support their effort who plan when to break away and when to shield the team leader. Strategy depends on the performance of your rivals and what you believe they can do in the rest of the race.

A good example of race strategy in action is the fable of the hare and the tortoise. The hare puts in effort early on and takes a huge lead. The hare then decides there is no point expending unnecessary effort in finishing the race quickly, and so allows the tortoise to catch up. Strategically, the hare's plan is a good one. The greater the hare's lead at any one point, the greater the effort required of the tortoise to win, and the lower the probability of succeeding. As our chances to win recede, most of us become discouraged and conserve effort, preferring to fight another day. The hare, unfortunately, makes two mistakes. First, it fails to recognize the commitment of the tortoise, who refuses to give up in the face of overwhelming odds. Second, and more importantly, the hare reduces effort by so much that it falls asleep, producing the improbable victory for the tortoise. The hare's failing is one of execution, not strategy. In real races, contestants who fall far behind often give up. In marathons, completing the course usually requires the athlete to take a rest before the next contest, while completing only half the course means a faster recovery. Thus a marathoner who is out of touch with the leader at the halfway stage often quits, preferring to race again sooner than would be possible by finishing. This is rational strategy for the contestant, but a problem for the race organizer, who wants to stage a thrilling race. As a result, organizers of marathons often award substantial second prizes, prizes for completion, and prizes based on time rather than order of finish, all of which help to keep contestants in the race until the end.

Objectives and Uncertainty of Outcome

Thus far we have assumed, along with Tullock and his followers, that the organizer's objective is to maximize effort. In a "symmetric" contest—one where all contestants have identical objectives and identical ability—the typical winner-take-all contest causes all the entrants to make the same effort. This means that the winner tries just as hard as any other contestant. But if contestants have different abilities or different objectives (some contestants may value the prize more than others or find it more costly to produce effort), then they may supply different effort levels in equilibrium. Under these circumstances, what would the contest organizer want to maximize: winning effort? Aggregate effort? Or something else entirely? In most competitions spectators are attracted by record-breaking feats, which might lead one to think that placing all the reward on winning effort makes sense. But as the discussion of second prizes suggested, winning effort might be maximized by giving a range of prizes, depending on the abilities of the contestants. Moreover, winning effort is not quite the same as breaking records, as can be seen in indoor cycling, where the riders often go as slow as they can for most of the race, producing a sprint only at the very end. Organizers can offer prizes based on timings to avoid this kind of strategic behavior.

In the end, contest organizers have to decide what their customers want and construct the incentives appropriately. In some kinds of competition, such as the Olympic Games, the issues seem straightforward. "Citius, Altius, Fortius," the motto of the Olympic movement (meaning "faster, higher, stronger"), just about sums up the objective of the organizers, and this is just what the spectators seem to want. While many decry the national medal tables associated with the games, many of the spectators see the Olympics as competition between nations, and the competition is structured so as to provide what the spectators want. The only difficulty in the design of this competition is what is acceptable competition and what is not. Doping, which has become such a huge problem for so many modern sports, stems from the winner-take-all incentive structure of competition. Monitoring compliance with the rules is so difficult and so uncertain that many commentators have argued that the athletes should be allowed to do whatever they want to themselves. We will return to this issue in chapter 4.

For competitions less prestigious than the Olympics, attracting spectators is a complex problem. Organizers of athletic meetings have typically struggled to attract spectators and TV interest. In the past promoters tended to focus on record breaking as a way to attract attention— perhaps the most famous example was the staging of Roger Bannister's assault on the four-minute mile in 1954. To stage such an event a promoter has to focus on the person who might break the record, rather than assembling a competitive field. Indeed, in some cases the organizer might have to pay a substantial appearance fee to the athlete while agreeing not to invite rivals. This is another illustration of the point that effort decreases with the number of contestants, and that prizes are often inefficient ways to achieve objectives. If the objective is to get an athlete of known talent to supply maximum effort, the best incentive is a fixed fee for entry and a bonus based on absolute, rather than relative, performance.

Attracting spectators by staging attempts on world records, however, is also relatively inefficient. Records are broken infrequently, and few events can credibly promise to deliver. Organizations such as the International Association of Athletics Federations (IAAF) have tried to build a program of regular events and to promote competition between the athletes themselves as the focus of spectator interest. To do this they have created rankings and championships running over a season, trying to stimulate a continuing interest in the progress of athletes. In essence, of course, this is exactly what leagues do for team sports— they provide a regular framework within which the performance of individual teams can be followed and supported.

Leagues work particularly well for team sports because spectators tend to maintain an attachment to a given team over a season, over a period of years, or over an entire lifetime. The 2005 film *Fever Pitch* portrayed the life of an obsessive Red Sox fan, and as in the film many fans see their entire lives wrapped up in the support of their team, in good times and in bad. This is different from an Olympic contest, where the spectators are only interested in the winner. In a league all the teams win some of the time, even if only one champion is crowned at the end of the season. The question for the league organizer is this— what makes for the most exciting championship race? The most common response is that it should be well balanced, meaning that many teams have a good chance of winning.

The idea that a well-balanced contest is essential to the success of a league has been advanced by league clubs themselves more or less from their inception. As far back as 1889 the National League claimed that the purpose of the reserve rule, which tied players to their clubs, was "a check upon competition," and that it had been instigated by the "weaker clubs." It was not until the 1950s that economists analyzed this claim systematically, at a time when organized baseball was coming under pressure from Congress and players' unions. The first important article on the economics of sport is usually considered to be Simon Rottenberg's essay on the baseball players' labor market, and the second to be Walter Neale's article on the "peculiar economics" of professional sports. These two articles, focused primarily on the organization of league sports, started from the assumption that the owners of clubs participating in a league seek to maximize profits. Rottenberg argued that even if teams liked winning, they would prefer to win by small margins rather than large ones. Therefore the distribution of talent throughout a league would tend to be relatively equal even if some clubs were much wealthier than others. Neale put the case even more strikingly: he pointed out that whereas in every other business

enterprise monopoly is the most profitable market structure, in the sports business monopoly is disastrous because
the monopolist will have no one to play against:

> Suppose the Yankees used their wealth to buy up not only
> all the good players but also all of the teams in the Ameri-
> can League: no games, no receipts, no Yankees. When, for
> a brief period in the late fifties, the Yankees lost the cham-
> pionship and opened the possibility of a non-Yankee World
> Series they found themselves—anomalously—facing sport-
> ing disgrace and bigger crowds. . . . "Oh Lord, make us
> good, but not that good," must be their prayer.

The essence of this argument is that the fans prefer to
watch a close contest rather than a predictable one—an
argument usually termed the "uncertainty-of-outcome
hypothesis." The hypothesis can take many forms. At its
simplest, a match involving two teams where everyone
expects one team to win easily is less attractive than one
where opinion is divided on the outcome. More broadly,
fans are likely to prefer a league competition where many
teams remain in contention rather than one with a run-
away winner. Taking an even longer perspective, a championship that many different teams succeed in winning
over the years is likely to be more attractive than one
where the same team, or a small clique of teams, tends to
win year after year.

There is one sense in which uncertainty of outcome
clearly matters—fans will generally not pay to watch the
same game twice. Unlike movies or music, once the viewer
knows the outcome the value of the product vanishes.
There are, of course, a few classic games in any sport that
people will pay to watch again on DVD, but these are few

and far between. Sports programming, which takes up a large share of the TV schedules, is a kind of instant soap-opera, which starts afresh with every single game. Uncertainty or suspense is the core of its appeal.

The attractiveness of uncertainty of outcome to sports consumers can be measured empirically and there have been a large number of studies attempting to do so. Borland and Macdonald surveyed thirty-nine papers published between 1974 and 2003 that examined whether fans responded to uncertainty. Most of these studies concentrated on either "match" uncertainty or "seasonal" uncertainty (only two of the studies examined the effect of uncertainty in the longer run). In all of these studies the crucial research question has been how to measure uncertainty. Match uncertainty studies have relied either on measures derived from historic performance to estimate the likely probability of each side winning or market-based estimates derived from betting. Betting odds might sound like the most reliable indicator, since the odds should reflect the balance of opinions among those interested in the outcome. However, the odds available in some leagues, such as English football, are fixed in advance by bookmakers and do not respond to the way in which betting (and therefore opinion) evolves in the run-up to the game. Estimating probabilities based on observable evidence such as past performance and the quality of the teams might produce an accurate estimate, so long as all relevant facts are taken into account (something that is hard to guarantee). Thus both types of study have their drawbacks. Out of eighteen studies examined by Borland and Macdonald, only four produced results suggesting that greater uncertainty of outcome generates greater demand to attend games—the remaining studies produced either insignificant results or even suggested that greater uncertainty reduced attendance.

Studies of seasonal uncertainty of outcome produced slightly stronger results, but were still surprisingly inconclusive. Seasonal uncertainty can be measured in a variety of ways, the most common being the number of games behind the leading team. Teams that are far behind in the championship might be expected to lose support since they are falling out of contention. Ten out of the nineteen studies Borland and Macdonald examined produced an unambiguous result suggesting that being in contention increased attendance at games, but nearly half of the studies produced results that were statistically insignificant or ambiguous. Given that there have been so few studies of the impact of long-term uncertainty, it is harder to reach any conclusion, but the signs are that any effects are weak and inconsistent.

These results represent one of the most surprising findings in the field of sports economics. It seems so intuitively plausible that uncertainty adds to the attractiveness of a league that it is hard to believe that empirical research does not strongly support this conclusion. Responses by economists have varied. Some have argued that the failure to find convincing results reflects problems in the analysis. Since many factors affect demand, it is difficult to isolate one on its own. The problem with this response is that uncertainty of outcome is not usually advanced as a minor factor, but as a key factor or even the biggest factor determining the demand for a sport.

The relative insignificance of uncertainty of outcome is perhaps most surprising in the context of North American sports, where, as we have seen, clubs have claimed for more than a century that it is critical, and where a whole host of collective measures, such as revenue sharing and salary caps, have been implemented in the name of improving competitive balance for the benefit of the fans.

Europeans, however, may be less surprised, especially if they follow one of the many successful national soccer leagues. Soccer has always been characterized by low uncertainty of outcome, especially in relation to championships. Thus, for example, out of seventy championships played in the official national soccer league championship of Portugal between 1938 and 2008, three teams have won sixty-eight times, despite the fact that dozens of teams have competed over the years. The three teams are Benfica, Sporting Lisbon, and Porto, and these teams are so big relative to their rivals that they usually occupy the top three spots in any season. Yet despite this Portugal's national league thrives up to the present day. Nor is this an unusual story in Europe. In Italy, the league is usually dominated by AC Milan, Internazionale, and Juventus, in Spain by Real Madrid and Barcelona. In Germany, Bayern Munich has won far more league titles than any other team, while over the last thirty years the English national league has been dominated by Liverpool, Manchester United, and Arsenal. The important point is that not only are these leagues unbalanced, but they are also very popular, and do not seem to suffer loss of consumer interest despite their relative predictability.

What is it that sustains interest in European soccer when it is dominated by a small number of teams? In addition to outcome uncertainty, two other factors contribute to demand for a sporting event. First, an important aspect is quality. Even if a team has lousy players, fans may still come to watch the visiting team. Some team owners have even built a business strategy around this idea, spending little on their own team and relying on the stars of rival teams to fill the stadium. Thus an uneven contest can attract fans, even though the outcome is predictable. In an unbalanced world it is possible to put together a dream team that will have universal appeal. Second, fans go to support their own team. Teams that win more often generate bigger support—but teams vary in the sensitivity of attendance to wins. For some teams, fans turn up come what may, while for other teams fans only turn up when the team is winning. One might expect that those teams whose fans are sensitive to wins will invest more than teams whose fans are not. As a result, competition can become quite unbalanced, but attendance overall can be quite healthy.

Cooperatives and Vertical Separation

I suggested above that the league format emerged as a good format for generating competition. By and large it was the clubs themselves that hit upon this idea, and set about organizing themselves into leagues. Economists have struggled to define the relationship between clubs in a league. The word *monopoly* has been frequently used, and Rodney Fort and James Quirk have stated trenchantly, "Professional team sports leagues are classic, even textbook, examples of business cartels." Clubs themselves don't relish the word *cartel*, with its implication of anti-competitive conduct, and argue that they are jointly suppliers of a league product. This idea, sometimes referred to as the single-entity doctrine, views the clubs as necessary collaborators who supply nothing alone. A more balanced view has been suggested by Michael Flynn and

Richard Gilbert, who argue that a league is a joint venture among the clubs. In a joint venture, the venture itself acquires its own personality, while the contributors to the venture are still independent entities.

Defining the relationship between the teams in a league is crucial because of the role played by competition law in defining what kinds of business organization are permitted. As club owners and managers see it, they agree to the rules of the league (which they consider to be their product), and therefore any agreement among themselves is simply as an arrangement to improve the quality of the product. On this view, restricting economic competition can be justified as a means to achieving some league-wide benefit, and the most commonly cited benefit has been competitive balance, which in turn relies on the concept of uncertainty of outcome. Critics believe that such arguments mask the true motive of the clubs, which is to maintain a cartel for the purposes of generating larger profits than would be possible in the face of economic competition. It is important here to distinguish sporting competition—rivalry on the field—from economic competition—rivalry for economic profit. These issues are discussed in more detail in the next chapter. For the time being, however, it is enough to note that our understanding of consumer demand for sports events, our understanding of the nature of a sports league, and our understanding of the objectives of clubs are all intimately connected. We could imagine, for example, a group of clubs pursuing the best interests of the sport by agreeing to keep up ticket prices and hold down wages, to produce a balanced competition among rivals so as to maintain a necessary uncertainty among the fans. Or we could imagine a group of profit-maximizing clubs organizing a cartel to maintain high prices and pay low wages under the cover of a supposed benefit in terms of competitive balance. Of course, these issues would be much easier to address if we had unambiguous results on the impact of uncertainty of outcome on demand, but unfortunately the evidence can be interpreted in support of either of these extreme positions, and anything in between.

Setting aside the issue of uncertainty of outcome, what is the appropriate organizational structure for a league competition? This chapter began by considering the provision of incentives for contestants by an independent competition organizer, while in practice most leagues are operated by the member clubs, who decide how the championship will be run. In general, there seem to be very different incentive structures adopted depending on the organizational form. In sports where the first kind of system is employed, such as tennis and golf, we tend to see the use of high-powered incentives—large prizes awarded to winners and significant financial incentives for performance. For example, since 1979 players on the Professional Golfers' Association (PGA) tour win prize money for each event according to a fixed formula, with 18 percent of the purse going to the winner, 10.8 percent going to second place, 6.8 percent to third place, and so on right down to seventieth place, which receives 0.2 percent. In league sports run by the clubs, money prizes are more or less unheard of. Teams generate revenue from selling tickets to their fans, but rather than paying this revenue into a pot and distributing according to success in the league, each team keeps its own revenue. Of course, one might argue that this revenue truly belongs to the club that invested in developing its local market. But even when there is collectively generated revenue (through the sale of broadcast rights, for example) this money tends to be distributed on the basis of equal shares independent of performance.

Would leagues benefit from introducing sharper incentives to achieve success? There are really two ways to look at this. One might ask whether there is a difference between "the good of the clubs and their owners" and "the good of the fans." Owners who compete more intensively to win are likely to make smaller profits, and this may explain why decisions taken by votes of owners do not tend to produce high-powered incentives, even if fans would like them. On this view organizational choices are about distributing the benefits produced by the league organization. On the other hand, one might question whether collective decision-making produces outcomes that are efficient for all concerned. Economic efficiency relies on the idea that all potential economic gains are recognized— this is not merely a question of distribution of benefits, but whether the maximum feasible benefits are being realized.

Collective decision-making can often be inefficient, as any family that has tried to organize a weekend outing through democratic voting can attest. Negotiations in collective decision-making are time-consuming, and any attempt to adjust to changing opportunities runs into this problem—consider how long it takes Congress or the United Nations to reach a decision. Moreover, decisions that require a majority frequently fall afoul of blocking coalitions, where those who have something to lose prevent a generally good idea from being accepted. This is especially common when new rules require a "supermajority," such as 66 percent of the vote, as is often the case with league rules. The problem is that collective rules tend to be established to make sure that no one member can be adversely affected, rather than maximizing the collective good. When it comes to defending political rights, this makes a lot of sense, but when it comes to good business decisions, such conservatism tends to block improvements. In general, businesses thrive by adapting rapidly to new opportunities rather than doing things the way they have always been done.

In economic terms, a sports championship can be thought of as two separate businesses, an upstream business of competition organizing, which involves the creation of a tournament format, the provision of incentives, arbitration procedures for disputes, and so on, and a downstream competition business, where clubs supply teams for competition within the established championship format. In sports like golf and tennis these functions are generally separated, while in team sports like Major League Baseball these functions are integrated and all decisions are controlled by the competitors themselves—the business is said to be "vertically integrated." Whether or not vertical integration produces efficiency is an interesting question. One way to think of this issue is to imagine all the owners in MLB selling the upstream business of league management to an independent organization that would run the league, while the owners continued to be responsible for running their franchise. If vertical integration were inefficient, the total market value of the downstream franchises and the upstream competition organizer would be greater than the aggregate value of MLB franchises at present.

In a sense, MLB long ago recognized the inefficiency of collective decision-making when it appointed a commissioner, a step that has been followed by all the other

U.S. major leagues. In the case of MLB, the need to appoint someone who could impose authority on the clubs arose out of the Black Sox scandal of 1919—the clubs recognized that the public would not trust them to sort out their own mess. The first commissioner, Judge Kenesaw Mountain Landis, insisted that he had been granted complete authority over baseball by the owners and imposed his iron will accordingly. When appointing commissioners since then, the owners have chiseled away at the remit of the job, effectively reasserting their own autonomy. Commissioners have played a large role in shaping other major league sports, most notably the NFL, where the role of the commissioner in forging agreements that benefit the league as a whole has been fundamental to making it one of the most successful sports leagues in the world.

In Europe a separation between club and league organization has always existed, given the role of the governing body in sports such as soccer. In most countries, the governing body existed first, and leagues were subsequently formed under the jurisdiction of the governing body. Thus while day-to-day league management has generally been maintained by the member clubs, the governing body has frequently been able to impose rules and regulations, ostensibly in the interest of the game as a whole.

Promotion and Relegation

There are many ways in which European soccer leagues differ from the North American major leagues, but one of the biggest differences is the institution of promotion and relegation. While the concept was developed by the clubs themselves, it seems likely that they wanted to maintain their good standing with the governing body and to be seen as an inclusive organization.

Promotion and relegation are not directly in the interests of clubs at the highest level—at best, the top clubs have to compete to maintain their position in the league, and at worst, they can plummet down the leagues. In England, for example, there are four main professional divisions (plus many other semipro divisions connected via promotion and relegation), and over a twenty-year period 95 percent of teams experience either promotion or relegation, nearly 50 percent experience life in three different divisions, and over 10 percent of teams visit all four. Given that teams in the top division play to audiences currently averaging around 35,000 per game, while teams in the fourth tier play to audiences of around 4,000, the slings and arrows of outrageous fortune can be piercing. On several occasions the top clubs have whispered the idea that the system could be done away with, but most fans view it as sacrosanct. No less an authority than the European Commission described the system as "one of the key features of the European model of sport."

Fans like the system since it gives every team, even the weaker ones, an opportunity to reach the highest level, and because it creates a thrilling end to the season not only at the top but also at the bottom. Moreover, fans can be confident that their club will be willing to invest in players, if only to avoid the threat of relegation. In short, the promotion and relegation system represents the kind of high-powered prizelike incentives that one might expect a contest designer interested in maximizing effort to adopt. With many European clubs facing severe financial crises in recent years, some have questioned the capacity of the leagues to sustain this system over the longer term.

There are many considerations to be taken into account in the design of a contest. These issues are important for organizers and for contestants. Given the importance spectator sports have in many peoples' lives, there is debate in the media about the agreements that the participants make among themselves. Moreover, it is not surprising that politicians sometimes get involved in debates that are close to the hearts of constituents. But over the years perhaps the most important public debates over the organization of sports are the ones that have taken place in the courts, and these have had to do with the legitimacy of economic agreements between the participants in sporting contests about the distribution of the spoils.

Three

SPORTS AND ANTITRUST

In December 1990 the Major League Baseball team owners agreed to pay $280 million in damages to the Players Association in compensation for colluding to undermine free agency. Between 1985 and 1988 the owners had apparently followed a tacit rule according to which no one would bid for a free agent until his prior club indicated that it was not interested in bidding. In 1985 only one out of twenty-nine free agents received an offer from another club *before* his former club had indicated that it would not bid. In the investigations that followed, no direct proof was ever offered that the owners had an explicit agreement to this effect; it was enough that the pattern of offers was strikingly predictable—after all, the owners met often enough to agree that such discipline in bidding would be in their financial interest.

This example raises a number of questions. First, is it right to apply concepts such as antitrust law, which was designed with commercial businesses in mind, to sporting enterprises? Second, if team owners run the league, and therefore have to meet with each other to agree on common issues such as the rules, where does one draw the line between a legal and an illegal agreement? Third, if sport deserves special treatment, should it be handed out on a case-by-case basis, or should sport be granted a general antitrust exemption?

In fact, sports leagues are widely viewed as monopolies, and as a result they seem to be almost constantly in litigation. In the words of Michael Flynn and Richard Gilbert, "One is struck by the frequency with which the structure and rules of professional sports leagues have been the subject of antitrust challenges in recent decades." To understand these issues it is first necessary to grasp the basics of antitrust law. Thus this chapter begins by summarizing how antitrust law works in general, and then examines how it is applied to the special case of sports.

Economics, Monopoly, and Cartels

Modern economies are built around markets. The market is a mechanism for organizing the production and exchange of goods and services, and ever since the days of Adam Smith economists have contended that free markets, in the sense that anyone can buy and anyone can sell, in any manner and at any price they choose, will function efficiently. The fundamental insight of Adam Smith is an example of the law of unintended consequences: "It is not from the benevolence of the butcher, the brewer, or the baker that we expect our dinner, but from their regard to their own self-interest." Competition among butchers, brewers, and bakers produces a ready supply of the products that we want to consume at the lowest possible prices. If this were not so, then an opportunity would exist for a supplier to introduce a new product or offer lower prices on existing products, and in free markets no profit opportunity is left unexploited. In this sense the benefit that we derive from the operation of the market relies not merely on what our supplier does for us, but what an alternative supplier could do for us. Monopoly is the situation where there is but one supplier, and no possible alternative.

Monopoly leaves the buyer at the mercy of the seller. Under a monopoly, the seller can make a take-it-or-leave-it offer, knowing that the buyer will have to go without if the offer is rejected. Monopoly is power, and monopoly brings a guaranteed profit. It is therefore not surprising that through the ages monopoly power has been prohibited in one way or another. To be more precise, the exercise of monopoly power has been almost entirely reserved for the state. States, through national governments, monopolize services such as the supply of money or the national defense. The state monopolizes the licensing of the airwaves, levels of air pollution, and the supply of new drugs. In some countries the state monopolizes other services such as the supply of education, hospitals, or electric power. In all such cases the state exercises this monopoly power in the name of people, claiming to use it to enhance the public good.

However, whenever monopoly power resides in private hands, there is a presumption that it will be used for private profit, and therefore it is either closely regulated or subject to prosecution. Regulation of monopoly can be seen at work in many sectors of the economy. Those services we refer to as utilities, such as power supply, water, and telephones, have typically been run by large corporations that are often the sole suppliers to large sections of the national population. In countries that decide private ownership is preferable to state ownership, private corporations face regulation over many aspects of their conduct. Typically regulation affects not merely prices, which are fixed at maximum levels, but also the quality of supply and the obligation to meet reasonable demands of customers. Regulation of monopoly is complex, precisely because there are so many ways to exploit a monopoly. The monopolist's weapon of choice is price—charging high prices across the board and the highest prices for those willing to pay the most. Thus regulators fix maximum prices, and oblige monopolists to charge all customers the same. Fixing price alone, however, only invites the monopolist to increase profits by reducing quality (and therefore costs). Specifying quality is in general much more difficult than specifying price, and therefore regulation can become intrusive, in the sense that managers of the monopoly find that almost any decision they make requires regulatory approval.

Regulation is usually adopted only when competition is not feasible. Utilities generally have significant economies of scale, meaning that competition carries a large cost penalty. For example, in most cities water is supplied by a single company that is responsible for the large network of pipes. Competition is not feasible simply because of the cost of duplicating this network—no company would consider laying a second set of pipes in order to compete with the incumbent supplier. Moreover, since the relevant monopoly is over the supply to an individual household, there would be no gain to splitting up the monopoly into two smaller ones—since each customer would remain the captive of its particular supplier. In splitting up a network the result would mostly be a duplication of costs. The crucial aspect of this logic is the absence of potential competition. Industries with very few suppliers can have very competitive prices so long as there exists potential competition. In such cases the threat of competition can be enough to keep a lid on prices. Without that threat, a monopolist is in a position to keep prices high and extract excessive profits.

Why should a monopolist's profits be considered excessive? The answer is not as obvious as it seems. The layperson's answer is that prices are too high—but this simply begs the question of what a fair price might be. Buyers always want to pay less, and sellers want to charge more. Put another way, profit is not generally considered evil in itself, or at least those people who do consider it so have a very particular view of how society should be organized, and it seldom includes a free market. Adam Smith's dictum suggests that profits are a good thing, since they induce butchers, brewers, and bakers to meet the needs of consumers. Indeed, some people take the view that high prices are a good thing in that the profits will be better used by the capitalist, who will reinvest in the business, than the consumer, who will just spend on consumption. But one does not have to take this view to see that "high prices" in themselves are not necessarily evil.

The economist's critique of monopoly profit rests on the notion of efficiency. If a monopolist charges a single price for all transactions, that single price will be significantly in excess of costs. Facing a uniform price, some consumers, who would be willing to pay a price that exceeds the monopolist's cost but not as high as the uniform price, will be excluded from the market. This is inefficient because even the monopolist would like to sell to them. This paradox arises if we assume that the monopolist is obliged to offer a uniform price and to sell to all customers at that price (a discount for some has very different implications for profit than a discount for all). Were the monopolist free to charge every consumer a different price—a practice known as "price discrimination"—then the inefficiency would no longer exist, and every consumer willing to pay more than the cost of production would be supplied with the product (this is equivalent to the monopolist charging a single price equal to the maximum that anyone would ever pay, and then offering each customer the smallest personal discount that would persuade them to buy, so long as the personal price exceeded the monopolist's production cost). Team owners frequently complain that building a stadium is so unprofitable that it requires public subsidies. Notwithstanding this, they charge a vast array of prices for seats, from luxury boxes to restricted views, matching what they offer to customers' willingness to pay. Imagine how much more profitable a stadium would be if all customers could be charged exactly their maximum willingness to pay for a seat. In economics this state of affairs is called "perfect" price discrimination.

Perfection in this sense is stymied by two problems. First, while consumers differ in their willingness to pay, it's not easy to determine what this amount is. Even if the consumers know themselves, the customers willing to pay a lot in general refuse to reveal the truth (it's never a problem getting low-willingness-to-pay customers to tell the truth). Thus price discrimination is generally not feasible, or, where it is feasible, relies on finding incentives for consumers to reveal their "type" through their choice. Thus airlines differentiate their services (for example, business class and coach, full fare and restricted fare) largely to sort passengers into groups of high and low willingness to pay, so that they can charge them accordingly (business-class fares are often five to ten times more expensive than coach, even though the extra cost of business-class seats is only three or four times greater).

The second problem with price discrimination is one of fairness. More than almost anything else, consumers hate paying high prices for a service that others are getting for less. So strong is this feeling that legislators in most countries pass laws to make such discrimination illegal. Without the opportunity to price-discriminate effectively, the monopolist is obliged to charge more or less a uniform price to all customers, and since this price is significantly higher than cost, some customers are inefficiently excluded from the market. The economic loss associated with this exclusion is known as the deadweight loss. It can be measured as a sum of money, since it depends on the number of consumers excluded from the market multiplied by the difference between the cost of supplying them and the monopoly price.[1]

In addition to the deadweight loss, monopoly can cause other problems. First, monopoly discourages innovation. Firms in competitive markets make small profits and therefore may gain from developing new methods or products, while a monopolist that already makes substantial profits has less to gain from a new idea. Monopolists may still innovate, but the incentives are not as sharp as they are for the competitive firm. Second, monopoly creates competition among potential sellers. Because monopoly is profitable, more people would like to be one, and

[1] There are some additional subtleties here that are dealt with in the economic textbooks. "Costs" in this context refers to marginal cost, that is, the extra cost of supplying marginal customers. For all customers, there are overhead costs, but since these are not directly attributable to individual customers they cannot be considered part of the marginal cost, and should therefore be excluded from the decision to supply. Overhead costs, however, must somehow be covered, and in the case of the monopoly there are many ways this could be done. Overheads could be divided on some basis among the buyers, but this just creates an inefficient gap between price and marginal cost. Alternatively the costs can be paid out of some kind of levy—but then it is not clear who should pay, or that the monopoly has the appropriate incentive to keep costs down. These kinds of arguments explain why the regulation of monopoly is ultimately a complex issue.

frequently governments choose to sell the license to be a monopoly. This can be a useful source of government revenue, but it can also be a source of revenue for politicians and public servants if they are willing to accept a bribe. Monopoly has a tendency to encourage corruption.[2]

Modern legislation against monopoly begins in the United States with the Sherman Act of 1890. Section 2 of the act states, "Every person who shall monopolize, or attempt to monopolize, or combine or conspire with any other person or persons, to monopolize any part of the trade or commerce among the several States, or with foreign nations, shall be deemed guilty of a felony." The language is careful not to make monopoly itself illegal. Every innovator who brings a new product to the market is by definition a monopolist, and such monopolies are highly desirable, so long as they give way to competition as new firms enter the market. What section 2 does is prohibit actions that can be construed as deliberately attempting to derail this process of competition—this is the meaning here of the word "monopolize." Hence in the famous recent antitrust case, Microsoft was accused of monopolizing the Internet browser market not because it wanted to be the biggest supplier in the market but because it wanted to prevent rivals from competing or entering the market.

[2]This can be seen in many countries around the world where bribery is the only way to obtain permits to engage in economic activities. In fact, this corruption also lay at the heart of the Statute of Monopolies passed in 1623 by the English Parliament. During her reign Queen Elizabeth had taken to selling official monopolies to raise money, and since she was always short of money, a considerable part of the economy was monopolized. Typically the monopolies were sold to her friends and supporters, who were thus able to become very rich at everyone else's expense. Parliament eventually persuaded her successor to outlaw the creation of such monopolies. This legislation is the ancestor of competition law not only in England but also in America, which at this time was just beginning to be colonized by the English.

It was accused of winning market share not by making a better product, but by creating barriers to competition.

Competition law did not follow in much of the rest of the world until after World War II. One reason for this gap in time is that the United States had to face up to the problem of monopoly power much earlier than most other countries. In Europe, which was industrializing in the nineteenth century in much the same way as the United States, the big difference was the fragmentation of the continent. Thus while the United States was opened up as one huge market by the railroads in midcentury, Europe remained artificially divided into separate markets by national boundaries and policies of protectionism. Faced with very small markets, very little competition was feasible in Europe. In the United States the competition created by the railroads led to the formation of business "trusts." Industrialists in a given line of business recognized that they could do better by agreeing to maintain high prices and divide up the country into exclusive territories.

Trusts were formed by businesses in industries such as sugar, steel, tobacco, and the railroads themselves. The most famous trust of all was created by John D. Rockefeller, in the form of Standard Oil, which at its peak controlled 90 percent of the U.S. oil refining industry. By putting together this trust Rockefeller was able to establish a near monopoly on what was already one of the most important commodities in the economy. Rockefeller was also one of the first victims of the Sherman Act, when the Supreme Court decided that Standard Oil had monopolized the industry and that the remedy for this abuse was breaking the company up into eleven independent, competing entities.

The Standard Oil Trust fell afoul of section 2 of the Sherman Act because it was an organization created out of competing refiners with the purpose of ending competition. However, it is also possible for competing firms to create agreements, possibly under contract, to fix monopolistic prices, and thereby share the profits of monopoly. Such actions are prohibited by section 1 of the Sherman Act, which states, "Every contract, combination in the form of trust or otherwise, or conspiracy, in restraint of trade or commerce among the several States, or with foreign nations, is declared to be illegal." Such conspiracies are in general termed *cartels*, and the common forms are typically price-fixing arrangements and bidding rings, whereby potential contractors agree to share business by allowing one of their members to offer the lowest (and yet still a monopoly) price.

There is an interesting difference between a monopolization case (Sherman Act section 2) and a cartel case (section 1). The concept of monopolization is about intent—what the intentions of the managers were when they engaged in particular activities. This naturally creates a lot of scope for legal argument, since intentions can only be inferred indirectly, not directly observed. By contrast, any agreement falling under section 1 is illegal. A cartel does not have to have been successful in achieving any particular goal in order for the members to be found guilty; merely joining the cartel is against the law. Moreover, the penalties for taking part in cartels nowadays are severe—managers are frequently sent to prison for their role in cartel agreements. Not surprisingly, therefore, the existence of cartels is hard to prove, since no one with any sense would keep a record of an illegal agreement. Nonetheless, cartel cases are not uncommon—they tend to arise in industries where a few firms dominate the market and have much to gain by agreeing to fix prices—examples include pharmaceutical companies, paper manufacturers, and steel producers.

Antitrust law elsewhere in the world is generally quite similar to the rules laid down in the United States. Europe did not introduce substantial competition laws until after the formation of the European Union in 1956, with its ambition to create a single European market. The European law prohibits "abuse of a dominant position" (which is akin to the rule against monopolization), and "all agreements between undertakings, decisions by associations of undertakings and concerted practices which may affect trade between Member States," in particular price fixing and market sharing (which is akin to the rule against conspiracies in restraint of trade). In recent years the media have focused on cases where European and American judges have reached different conclusions, but most experts agree that the similarities are far greater than the differences, and much the same can be said about other jurisdictions such as Japan and Australia. Even developing countries, which in the past were reluctant to adopt antitrust law (citing concerns about the viability of domestic producers in the face of foreign competition), have fallen into line following the adoption of global trade rules under the auspices of the World Trade Organization.

Sports Leagues as Monopoly Cartels

In chapter 2 we referred to a famous statement about the economic status of American sports leagues: "Professional team sports leagues are classic, even textbook, examples of business cartels." The rationale for this judgment is straightforward. Organizations such as Major League Baseball and the National Football League dominate their sports. There is no credible competition from rival leagues. In each sport there are minor leagues and varsity competitions, which in some cases draw significant crowds, but none of these pose a real competitive threat. The major leagues possess market power in the sense that they can sustain prices well above competitive levels without fans deserting them for rival competitions and without new leagues entering the market.

Now, the leagues themselves might dispute this contention. To establish in a court of law that a business has market power requires both a definition of the market and proof that the operations of the business in that market are not constrained by competition, actual or potential. Market definition is nowadays thought of in terms of the SSNIP test (pronounced "snip test"). SSNIP stands for a "small, significant and nontransitory increase in price," and a relevant market is defined by the smallest set of producers such that these producers could collectively impose a small, significant, and nontransitory increase in price, over and above the competitive price level, and thereby increase profitability. The size of price increase is usually thought of as something in the region of 5 percent. Major League Baseball is a relevant market in this sense if we suppose that a 5 percent price increase above the minimum competitive level (not the actual level), imposed collectively by the owners, would be profitable.

Do the owners make money? Owners themselves claim to lose money, but a host of specialist sports economists, including Roger Noll, Andrew Zimbalist, Rodney Fort, and James Quirk have shown that, once all relevant sources of revenue are accounted for, the major leagues are truly profitable. The ever-escalating value of franchises seems to suggest that profits are being made somewhere, even if they are not visible to the naked eye. There are many ways owners can conceal profits if they want to. For example, they can overstate amortization of assets, they can make unnecessary payments to other companies they own, and they can overpay themselves. These methods are sometimes helpful in reducing the owner's tax bill, and sometimes helpful in negotiating with player unions. But economists are convinced that on average major league franchises generate substantial profits. Many attribute these profits to rapidly rising prices that are set well above competitive levels. On this basis, each major league sport can be considered a market in its own right.

Of course, if this is true, then by definition a major league is a monopoly and the owners acting collectively possess monopoly power. Moreover, the threat that this monopoly will be challenged by the entry of new major leagues seems remote. Historically, there have been some attempts to set up rival new leagues. Indeed, the National League faced a number of entrants in the nineteenth century—the American Association in the 1880s, the Union League, the Players League in 1890, and in 1901 the American League. In each case entry led to savage competition, price cutting, and big salary increases for players. In every case but the last, only the National League was left standing. When it became clear that the American League could not be beaten, it was co-opted, creating the structure that we now call Major League Baseball. Following the failure of the Federal League in baseball, there have been no attempts at entry that have gotten beyond the drawing board. Professional leagues in American football came later and took longer to settle down. The National Football League, founded in 1920, faced a number of rivals at different times, most of which were called the American Football League. League competition finally ended in 1966 when the NFL merged with the fourth incarnation of the AFL, and since then three significant attempts to enter the market have failed—in 1975 (the World Football League), 1985 (the United States Football League), and XFL in 2001.

While their histories are complex, similar conclusions can be drawn with respect to the evolution of the National Basketball Association and the National Hockey League: any new entry is typically doomed to economic failure, while any sign that the entrant might succeed leads to co-option into the monopoly, either of the league as a whole or of selected teams. The reasons for economic failure are also not hard to find. An entrant league usually competes by creating teams in cities that have been excluded from the existing league. However, any successful entrant also needs a presence in some of the major cities such as New York, L.A., and Chicago, where the incumbent is already established. The incumbent tries to squeeze the entrant hardest where there is head-to-head competition, pushing prices down so that the rival franchise is unprofitable, while itself adding teams in some of the markets where the entrant had hoped to have the only franchise. The incumbent strategy has seldom failed, and therefore entry seems not to be an effective constraint on the monopoly power of the major leagues.

There is, of course, no dispute that the owners of the major league teams explicitly collude. Unlike most cartels, which are cloak-and-dagger affairs, the management committee of a league meets frequently and openly so that owners can discuss their plans. All major policies are decided by a majority vote of the owners. Surely the activities of the owners fall afoul of section 1 of the Sherman Act?

The Competitive Balance Defense

William Hulbert, founder of the National League and creator of the business model for American professional league sports, was an experienced member of the Chicago Board of Trade. He turned baseball from a sport run by its players into a business run by businessmen. The nature of owning a team changed and so did the personalities; in the words of David Voigt, "One sees few of the convivial gentlemen sponsors after this year [1878]; in their place there now emerged the impersonal, profit-seeking owner type." These new men knew a thing or two about how to run a trust. They understood that, from a business point of view, clubs needed an incentive in developing their fan base, and hence they mandated exclusive territories. They also understood that competition between clubs for the best players would wipe out profits, and hence they invented the reserve rule. Nothing better illustrates the shift in the control of the game from players to owners. The rule stated that each club could designate players at the end of each season who could not sign with any other club without their owner's permission. The rule effectively tied a player to a club as long as it still wanted him. Originally the rule applied to five players only, but soon it was expanded to eleven, and in 1907 to all players under the uniform contract. In this way the employer held a monopoly right over the baseball services of the player (of course, the reserve rule placed no restriction on a player becoming an actor or a brain surgeon). Economists term this situation "monopsony"; baseball players called it slavery. Players might object to the restriction on their freedom of choice, but the most practical effect was to hold down players' wages. If businesses such as Ford and General Motors tried to impose such a rule on their employees, they would quickly find themselves in court and convicted of operating a cartel.

When the rule was introduced in 1879 the National League issued a statement explaining that the clubs were losing money and proposed the rule as the solution because "the principal cause of heavy losses to [NL clubs] is attributed to high salaries, the result of competition." In other words the rule was a means to raising profits. Today, any business presenting this argument in court would instantly be found guilty of an antitrust violation, and the only question would be the size of the damages to be paid. No matter how much money a business is losing in a competitive market, collusion to keep costs down at someone else's expense is against the law. But in 1879 the law did not exist.

By 1889, however, it was becoming clear that Congress would limit the activities of trusts and cartels and so the National League started to present a rather different rationale. In 1889, faced with competition from the Players League, the National League offered the following statement to explain the reserve rule: "As a check on competition, the weaker clubs in the League demanded the privilege of reserving five players." This is perhaps the first case in history of the competitive balance defense. The significance of the defense was not immediately obvious. At the time, the reserve rule was credited with bringing stability to the league and hence benefiting fans and even the players. Challenges by the players tended to involve the legality of the contract itself and its restrictions on the player, rather than any attack on the league as a monopoly or cartel. As a result the player usually lost, since, according to the legal doctrine of the day, his contract was valid since willingly entered into.

The first antitrust challenge to the monopoly of the National League and American League—what was then known as "organized baseball"—came as a result of the failure of the Federal League in 1915. Baltimore, one of the bankrupt Federal League clubs, sued under the Sherman Act, claiming that the reserve rule helped the clubs of organized baseball to monopolize the sport. This case culminated in one of the most important and controversial rulings in the world of sports litigation. The case was eventually referred to the Supreme Court, which ruled in 1922 that because baseball games were played within each state, it did not involve interstate commerce, and therefore federal law, which includes the Sherman Act, did not apply. Bizarre as it may sound (and most lawyers and judges have confirmed that this ruling makes little sense), the ruling effectively handed an antitrust exemption to organized baseball, rendering moot any further discussion of the rights and wrongs of the reserve rule.

After World War II, however, the mood changed and the operation of baseball and the other emerging professional sports started to come into question. By this time the rule had evolved into a clause in the standard one-year contract signed by every player, giving his club the option to renew the contract for one further year. Since each new contract contained the option clause, the player was effectively tied to the club as long as it wanted him. At a time of growing prosperity players argued that the reserve rule limited their employment opportunities and the chance to share in the growing affluence of baseball. The Supreme Court declined to overturn its own ruling despite admitting that it was not a very sensible one, and appealed to Congress to legislate. In 1951 Congress held lengthy hearings on the activities of organized baseball, at the center of which lay the reserve clause. The clubs claimed that without it chaos would ensue and the league would collapse. To make this argument they articulated more fully the competitive balance defense.

Among those giving testimony, including leading players, journalists, and owners, the committee found more or less unanimous support for the reserve clause. The committee's report states that "the principal reason advanced in support of this generally held opinion was that the reserve clause was needed to equalize competition among the various clubs within professional baseball leagues. Reasonable equality of competition is essential if spectator interest is to be maintained, and, of course, fan interest is needed if professional baseball is to be a financial success."

The competitive balance defense should properly be divided into three core propositions:

- A contest is more exciting the more uncertain the outcome, and therefore more attractive to fans.

- An uncertain outcome can only be produced if there is an even distribution of competitive resources among the contestants.

- An even distribution can be produced by sharing resources (for example, gate money or TV revenue) or by restricting the market for players (for example, restrictions on mobility, on team size, or wage payments).

We have already examined the first part, the uncertainty-of-outcome hypothesis, and found that there is limited statistical evidence to support it. Like most economic arguments, however, there are enough incidents that can be cited as examples of the hypothesis at work to satisfy many that what seems like a commonsense proposition is in fact true.

The second part of the defense has received only limited attention by researchers, but is in fact one of the most interesting aspects of the entire defense. It is one thing to accept that inequality of results is harmful to a sports league, quite another to suggest that measures to equalize the distribution of playing resources can remove this inequality. Implicit in this hypothesis is that results respond to the input of resources, or, more simply, that teams can buy success. This is a controversial proposition among fans, particularly fans of teams that have squandered big budgets with little apparent success. Some people believe that success cannot be bought, and that putting together a bunch of superstars does not create a winning team. There is something in this, in the sense that David sometimes defeats Goliath. The question is how often it happens. The proposition is quite easy to examine, since results are public knowledge and there is also plenty of data available on what teams spend.

Studies conducted in recent years show that there is a statistically reliable relationship between what teams spend and what they achieve on the field, but there are differences between sports. In MLB, for example, variation in the amount spent by a team from season to season, relative to its competitors, accounts for about one-quarter of the variation in a club's league performance from season to season. This may not sound like much, but it gives more of an edge to an individual team than any other single factor. Spending in the NBA or NHL can explain variation in performance to about the same degree. In the major European soccer leagues, however, spending on players accounts for a far larger share of the variation in results, often well over 50 percent. In the NFL, by contrast, variation in spending bears almost no relation to winning.

The reason we get these contrasting results is twofold. First, the relationship depends on the extent to which the market for players operates. If players are bought and sold regularly in a market, then just as in any other market, the prices tend to reflect accurately the value to the buyers, which is mostly measured in terms of success on the field. If markets are restricted from operating, then prices (wages) paid are less likely to reflect contributions (productivity), and therefore the correlation will be weaker. In European soccer there is a thriving national and international market in players, and therefore prices tend to reflect performance, while in the major leagues player markets tend to be more restricted, and therefore prices are less likely to accurately reflect productivity. Some people like to argue that causation might run in the other direction; rather than high wages buying a successful team, it is the success of the team that leads to high wages being paid out to winners. Clearly this is true to some extent, but in general players are paid fixed wages (for reasons we will discuss in the next chapter), with win bonuses accounting for only a small part of total remuneration. What players are paid reflects what their employers think they are worth, largely in terms of their ability to generate wins for the team. The statistical correlation between wins and team expenditure is therefore a measure of how good the team owners are at predicting performance.

The second factor determining the relationship between spending and performance is how much expenditure varies between the teams. If there is no variation in spending, then logically it is impossible for expenditure to explain any variation in team performance. This is precisely the situation in the NFL, where all teams spend almost exactly the same amount. This does not mean, of course, that if expenditure did vary, it would not explain variation in performance.

As a logical conclusion to the first two parts, the third part of the competitive balance defense is invoked by league organizations to justify the restraints they impose. We have already seen how baseball defended the reserve clause on these grounds. Baseball's reserve clause was finally overturned in 1976, but not in an antitrust court. In 1972 the players' union funded a challenge by Curt Flood, a .300 batter and talented outfielder who had suddenly found himself traded from the Cardinals to the Phillies at the age of thirty-one, very much against his will. Although the case went to the Supreme Court, it simply reaffirmed the antitrust exemption, while accepting that it made little sense. Instead, it was the process of collective bargaining with the union, and the acceptance by the owners of arbitration for grievances that destroyed the reserve clause. To understand this, it is important to recognize that labor relations in baseball were affected by the general political climate in the 1960s, which was more responsive to the interests of employees. Politicians saw negotiation between employers and unions as a way to maintain orderly industrial relations, and in the event of failure, encouraged independent arbitration as a way to settle disputes. With hindsight it seems odd that the baseball owners, with their unassailable monopoly, agreed to collective bargaining with the union. At the time the commissioner strongly opposed it, but the owners ignored his warnings and were, perhaps, guilty of overconfidence. Perhaps they didn't reckon on the independent thinking demonstrated by Peter Seitz, the arbitrator they agreed to.

If so, they were soon brought back to earth. Collective bargaining led to the end of what the owners had always believed to be a cornerstone of their business model. It all followed in the wake of Dodgers pitcher Andy Messersmith's amazing 1974 season in which he recorded nineteen wins and seven shutouts. When salary negotiations for the following season produced a deadlock, the Dodgers' owner, Walter O'Malley, invoked the reserve clause and renewed the contract with a small pay increase. 1975 was a rerun of 1974, and O'Malley tried to use the time-honored interpretation of the clause yet again. Thanks to the new collective bargaining agreement Messersmith was entitled to have the use of the reserve clause interpreted by the independent arbitrator, not a court. Of course, the arbitrator could have decided that the owners' interpretation was correct. But he didn't. He said that the one year specified in the initial contract meant precisely that—one year only, and this year expired with the end of the second one-year contract, leaving the player a free agent. With an arbitrator's decision almost inviolable, all that was left for the owners was to negotiate a new era of free agency. The subsequent attempt at collusion by the owners (mentioned at the beginning of this chapter) tried to preserve the clause by other means, but it only led to a multi-million-dollar settlement and all-around humiliation. Freedom can be a relative term—players only become free agents after seven years in the deal negotiated with the union, but from the 1980s onward players' salaries exploded. In 1980 the average team was paying $4 million per year in salaries; by 2006 it was paying over $90 million. Even after allowing for general price inflation, this was an extraordinary increase.

Of course, it is reasonable to believe that owners knew that free agency would increase salaries. But what about their argument that the reserve clause maintained competitive balance in baseball? Here is the verdict of Roger Abrams, a former MLB salary arbitrator: "The facts ... do not support sports team owners' claims that a reserve system maintains competitive balance. Under the comprehensive reserve system baseball had a history of dynastic, ruling clubs—Baltimore and Boston in the 1890s; the three New York City teams throughout much of the twentieth century; and the St. Louis Cardinals organization in the 1920s, 1930s, and 1940s, under the brilliant management of Branch Rickey. And some baseball clubs have remained perennial losers—the Chicago Cubs have not won a World Series since 1907, the Boston Red Sox since 1918[3] and the Cleveland Indians since 1948. The reserve system did nothing to enhance the competitiveness of these clubs."

Perhaps the most important argument advanced in the economics of sports went back to the earlier investigations of Congress in 1951. Simon Rottenberg, whose famous article was mentioned in the previous chapter, was the first economist to seriously consider the competitive

[3] The book was published in 1998.

balance defense. He argued that the reserve clause could be thought of as a property right over the revenue stream generated by a player allocated to the club, while under free agency the property right resided with the player. He then asked whether ownership of this property would affect the ultimate destination of a player in a competitive market. He concluded that it would not. Whoever owned the property right, there would be a tendency for that right to migrate to wherever it was most valued, since the owner, whoever he was, would want to maximize returns. This Rottenberg called the invariance principle.

The invariance principle is remarkably reminiscent of another famous proposition in economics, the Coase Theorem. George Stigler stated it thus: "With zero transactions costs, private and social costs will be equal"; in this context "private" means costs borne by a specific person or corporation, while "social" means the sum of all private costs. The significance of this statement, as Coase himself put it, is that "if private cost is equal to social cost, it follows that producers will only engage in an activity if the value of the product of the factors employed is greater than the value which they would yield in their best alternative use." In other words, resources naturally migrate to their most valuable employment, regardless of who owns them. The article in which Coase outlined his argument was only published in 1960, four years after Rottenberg's. In fact, it was Coase's idea that won him a faculty post at the University of Chicago, where Rottenberg was himself based. Whether Coase was aware of Rottenberg's work remains one of the intriguing puzzles of economic research in sport. Did events prove Rottenberg (and Coase) correct? If anything, competitive balance has *improved* since the ending of the reserve clause, although perhaps too many other things have changed for this fact to be considered a conclusive test.

Without a federal antitrust exemption, many restraints imposed by the other major league sports in the United States have been challenged, generally by the player unions that saw their members disadvantaged by restraints on the labor market. Perhaps the most famous labor market restraint after the reserve rule is the draft system, invented by the NFL, which allocates sole negotiating right with a new player entering the league to a single team. It is not hard to see how this reduces the player's bargaining power (and therefore salary), but by allocating priority according to the reverse order of finish in the league from the previous season, the NFL has been able to claim that the system was justified under the competitive balance defense. Sadly for the NFL, when the draft was considered by the courts in 1978 it was held to be an unreasonable restraint of trade. This was notwithstanding the fact that there is statistical evidence that the draft has enhanced competitive balance both in the NFL and in MLB.

As with many such restrictions, the fact that they might achieve the owners' stated end is not enough—the owners must also prove that there does not exist a less restrictive alternative. The adverse antitrust judgment has forced the owners into the arms of the player unions. In the United States there have been a number of statutory antitrust exemptions granted to unions for the purposes of maintaining labor relations. Essentially the logic is that if unions are to represent their members, they must do so on a collective (collusive) basis, and therefore antitrust cannot apply. Even when not covered by statute, courts have applied a nonstatutory exemption in order to maintain a consistent approach. Thus any restraint that a league can write into a collective bargaining agreement becomes immune from antitrust.

Such was the fate of the rookie draft. Salary caps, first applied by the NBA in the 1984–85 season, were also the product of negotiation with the players' union. The original salary cap stated that no team could spend more than 53 percent of defined average team revenues.[4] The economics of a salary cap are not so different from those of a draft; on the one hand both have a tendency to equalize opportunities and therefore increase competitive balance, while on the other hand both tend to reduce spending on the players. A salary cap unilaterally imposed by the owners would be as unlikely to survive an antitrust suit as the draft. The reason that unions agreed to these arrangements is that they were able to extract concessions such as increased contributions to insurance and retirement funds, as well as minimum salaries for lesser players. In economic terms these arrangements have benefited the owners and the majority of players at the expense of the relatively small number of star players.

This point became crystal clear in 1995 when some of the star players, including Michael Jordan and Patrick Ewing, tried to get the union decertified, so that the salary cap would no longer be covered by the labor exemption. Egged on by the owners, the majority of players, who could not expect to reach the Jordan income bracket, voted to keep the union and their minimum salaries. As a competitive balance measure the NBA salary cap was a hopeless failure, a fact amply demonstrated by the Chicago Bulls dynasty that won six titles out of eight between

---

[4] Since then both the percentage and the revenue base to which this is applied has changed; at the time of writing the percentage was 51% of a larger revenue base.

1991 and 1998. The main problem with the NBA cap has been that it permits too many exceptions to be considered a serious restraint on player spending.

A tougher version of the salary cap was introduced by the NFL (with union agreement) in 1994. The cap allowed a team to spend 63 percent of average league revenues, but permitted fewer exemptions and has thus been considered a "hard" rather than a "soft" cap. Nonetheless, NFL teams have shown themselves able to find their way around the cap, notably through the payment of signing bonuses that, while paid in full in year one of a contract, are prorated across the life of a contract for the purposes of calculating the cap. Assessing the contribution of the salary cap is difficult because the league encourages competitive balance in so many ways.

Besides the draft and the cap, there are roster limits (these are used by all the major leagues as a means to stop stockpiling of talent and have not been challenged under antitrust), gate revenue sharing (40 percent of designated gate receipts go to the visiting team in the NFL), sharing of merchandising income, and equal sharing of collectively sold broadcast revenue. Art Modell once famously joked of the NFL, "We're 26 Republicans who vote Socialist!" and the NFL is frequently cited as compelling evidence in support of the competitive balance defense.

So how balanced is the NFL? I mentioned earlier that bookmakers' odds are a good guide to what people believe about likely outcomes, and this applies to beliefs about competitive balance. Consider the betting odds for Super Bowl XLII. In September 2007 (before the regular season started) the clear favorite was the New England Patriots, with the odds implying that their probability of winning the Super Bowl was in the region of 20 percent (if a bookmaker offers you a return of $4 for every $1 you bet, the implied probability is $1 divided by $5 [consisting of $4 paid out plus your initial stake of $1 which the bookmaker returned to you], hence, the probability is one in five, or 20 percent). Outsiders such as the Cleveland Browns, the Oakland Raiders, or Houston Texans were being offered at odds that implied their probability of winning was in the range of 0.5 percent to 1 percent. If the NFL were perfectly balanced, then each of the thirty-two teams would have a one in thirty-two probability of winning—roughly 3 percent each. So the NFL does not sound like a perfectly balanced championship judging by the opinions of the betting public. The four most popular teams with bookmakers were jointly deemed to have a probability of over 50 percent of winning the Super Bowl.

In the event, Super Bowl XLII was won by the outsider New York Giants (whose chances were rated at the start of the season at between 1 percent and 3 percent). Up until that point, their opponents, New England, had enjoyed a perfect season (eighteen wins and no losses), only to lose in the Super Bowl by the narrow margin of 17–14. Moreover, Super Bowl XLII was recognized as a shock result (something that occurs in all sports). In the previous season the bookmakers had made the Indianapolis Colts the clear favorite at the start of the season (also with a probability of winning of around 20 percent), and they did in fact go on to win Super Bowl XLI. Bookmakers' odds guarantee nothing, but they are seldom far from the truth. As this book goes to press (September 2008) the four favorites for Super Bowl XLIII are New England, Indianapolis, the San Diego Chargers, and the Dallas Cowboys. Absent major injuries it would be surprising if one of these did not end up as winner, and extraordinary if at least one did not make it to Super Bowl XLIII.

One reason for this degree of predictability is the influence of a small number of key players in the team. In football the quarterback is the most influential player; currently Tom Brady (New England) and Peyton Manning
(Indianapolis) are dominant among quarterbacks; therefore their teams are also likely to dominate. However, the
rules that ensure that teams have equal opportunities to
hire new talent, notably the draft system, also ensures that
dynasties are short-lived. If you are the worst team in the
NFL today, the chances are you will get to pick a star
quarterback next year, and so will have a shot at the Super
Bowl in five years' time. Other leagues, such MLB, the
NBA, or European soccer leagues, have less reliable draft
systems, or no draft at all, and are therefore more prone
to dynasties. It is usually the emergence of dynasties that
provokes soul-searching about competitive balance.

The dominance of the New York Yankees in the second
half of the 1990s led the commissioner to form the Blue
Ribbon Panel on Baseball Economics in 1999. The panel
defined a proper level of competitive balance as a state
where "every well-run club has a regularly recurring hope
of reaching postseason play" and found that revenue dis-
parities among the teams were undermining competitive
balance in this sense. As a result the panel recommended
a significant increase in revenue sharing combined with a
mandatory minimum level of expenditure by each team.
These proposals weren't followed, but revenue sharing
was increased through the "luxury tax." This taxes teams
that spend above a fixed level and shares out the revenue
among the remaining teams. In any case the panel produced little evidence to demonstrate that attendance
at MLB was being adversely affected by competitive
imbalance.

So far the discussion has focused on self-evidently profit-oriented leagues and owners. Sporting bodies whose members can reasonably claim to be not-for-profit organizations sometimes imagine they are automatically exempt from antitrust laws, and so have no need of the competitive balance defense. This is not the case. Antitrust laws apply to almost any *economic* activity, regardless of the claimed motives of the monopolists or members of the cartel. Even amateur sports bodies fix ticket prices and sell broadcast rights, and so are covered by the law (after all, if all that were necessary to evade competition law were to claim a higher motive than profit, presumably all businesses would recast themselves as charities). The NCAA, which organizes college athletics in the United States, became embroiled with the antitrust laws in the 1980s. The NCAA is essentially a cartel for college and university athletics, since members are represented on its organizing committees. Up until this time the NCAA controlled the rights to broadcast college football games on TV and allowed only a small number to be shown. By restricting the number of games the NCAA deprived colleges of the opportunity to generate revenue, especially those with a football history. Oklahoma University challenged, under the Sherman Act, the right of the NCAA to prevent it from selling its games. In its defense the NCAA claimed that the restriction was necessary to preserve interest at games played by smaller colleges (otherwise fans would stay at home and watch the games of the big teams) and hence helped to preserve competitive balance. The NCAA lost the case because the court deemed the TV restraint too restrictive and because there was in fact very little balance in college football, even if the aim of promoting it was a legitimate objective. Collective selling of

TV rights has already been mentioned in relation to the NFL. In chapter 5 the issue of sport and broadcasting will be considered in more detail.

Most of the litigation surrounding the competitive balance defense has taken place in the United States. While the principal European soccer leagues have long matched their American counterparts in terms of social significance, only in very recent years has this significance been translated into economic power. We have already seen how the rules of the European league system discouraged profit-making activities and how the system of promotion and relegation undermined the opportunity to make profit. However, this did not mean the absence of restraints in the labor market.

In England the Football League introduced a system to control the movement of players that was very similar to the reserve rule almost from the start. Within one year (in 1889) of operating, there was a rule requiring the consent of the league to the transfer of a player, and it seems likely that, just as the notion of the league itself was copied from baseball, so the idea of restricting players' mobility also crossed the Atlantic. The system that ultimately emerged, known as the retain and transfer system, prevented any other league club from hiring a player without consent of his present club. As the system of governance spread both domestically and internationally, the freedom of movement of players was effectively controlled. As in the United States, early attempts to challenge this restriction in the courts failed on the grounds that a player had freely entered the contract. From the 1950s onward a series of government reports investigated the operation of the system, which, like their American counterparts, the league clubs claimed was necessary to the preservation of balance.

This was despite the fact that the soccer leagues in England and the rest of Europe have always been far more unbalanced than their American counterparts and dominated by a small number of clubs.

The retain and transfer system was overturned by an English court ruling in 1964, which held it to be an illegal restraint of trade. From that time on players gradually achieved a form of free agency, giving them the right to move to a new club if they wanted. In the American system, when a player moves to another club his existing contract is taken up by the new employer. Usually the club that the player is leaving is willing to contribute toward payment of the contractual wage. In the European system, however, the old contract is torn up and a new one signed when a player moves, and it has always been normal practice for the buying club to pay a fee, known as the transfer fee, to the selling club. Even when players in England won the right to move to a new club if they wanted to, payment of a transfer fee was still required, even if the player's contract had come to an end. While the size of the fee would ultimately be settled by an arbitration panel, the existence of these fees undoubtedly hindered players' mobility.

In the rest of Europe the system was closer to the one that existed in England prior to 1964, with employers having an absolute veto over the movement of players. The problem came to the attention of the European courts in 1995 in the form of the Bosman case. Jean-Marc Bosman was a Belgian playing for a Belgian team who wanted to transfer to a French club that was willing to pay a transfer fee. Under the rules of the Belgian Football Association the Belgian club had the right to veto the transaction without appeal (and so retain Bosman's services), which it did on the grounds that the buying club could not really afford the fee. Under the laws of the European Union citizens are guaranteed the right to transfer their labor freely between member states, and the European Court of Justice ruled that the existing transfer system violated this right. As a result the soccer federations of Europe were obliged to rewrite their rules to permit players to move freely between clubs once their contracts terminated. The court rejected the argument of the national associations that the transfer system helped to preserve competitive balance (or "solidarity," as the court called it), on the grounds that there was no obvious way in which the rule preserved it. The only other significant cases in Europe relating to the competitive balance defense have concerned broadcasting, and these will be mentioned in chapter 5.

Four

SPORTING INCENTIVES

Jose Canseco is proud to claim that he introduced the systematic use of anabolic steroids into baseball. The first player ever to hit forty home runs and steal forty bases in a season, he would probably have been a cinch for the Hall of Fame, absent some injuries and his boasts about steroids: "I was known as the godfather of steroids in baseball. I introduced steroids into the big leagues back in 1985, and taught other players how to use steroids and growth hormone." But Canseco is not repentant. First, he believes "every steroid out there can be used safely and beneficially." Second, he argues that taking steroids is simply "economics 101 . . . let's say you're a talented young player from an impoverished area of Puerto Rico or the Dominican Republic. And let's say you realize that, if you can put together back-to-back good seasons with strong home run totals, you can realistically set up your family and yourself for the rest of your life with a $40 to $50 million contract. There's only one catch: to score the big paycheck, to set up your family and become one of the richest people in your country or on your island, you're going to need to guarantee that performance—and the only way to ensure that is to make the most of the opportunity presented by steroids and growth hormone. Put it that way, I don't see any young kid turning it down. Would you? Would you really?"

Third, he argues that steroids are what the fans really want: "People want to be entertained at the ballpark. They want baseball to be fun and exciting. They are easy for even the most casual fan to appreciate. Steroid-enhanced athletes hit more home runs. So yes, I have personally reshaped the game of baseball through my example and my teaching." And there's more: "I am glad that soon enough the work I've done will reshape the way millions of you out there live your lives, too. Why should only top athletes with huge salaries reap the benefits of the revolution in biotechnology that will define our times? Why shouldn't everyone get to ride the wave?"

To which most of us would probably answer that the rewards don't outweigh the risks. Advocates like Canseco point out that if people understand very little about the real dangers of steroids, it is precisely because they are banned. He argues that steroids taken properly pose negligible risks—but there are known risks. These include stress to the heart, liver damage, irritability, and susceptibility to depression, while use by young people also creates risks of stunted growth and organ abnormalities. Yet even to make this argument is to cede Canseco's main point—steroid use is like consumption of alcohol or caffeine, just a question of risk and reward. In the sports world the extraordinary growth in rewards in recent decades has made all sorts of risks seem more palatable.

Modern professional sports are in the region of one hundred years old. Some, like baseball in the United States and soccer in England, go back a bit further, while others are surprisingly recent—for example, professional soccer in Germany did not start officially until 1963. Rugby union represents an extreme case where the sport existed in the nineteenth century but did not permit professionalism until 1995. Generally speaking, professionalism, meaning that the players are paid to play, comes only when the sport can generate enough revenue from spectators, merchandising, and the sale of broadcast rights to pay something more than the best alternative job players could take. The transition to professionalism is then a consequence of economic competition among those who want the services of the players—the clubs in the case of team sports and competition organizers in the case of individual sports. Collusion among club owners or competition organizers can resist the pressure to move to professionalism as a way to keep down costs, but such restraints are unlikely to survive antitrust laws. Only if some special principle can be invoked in defense of amateurism can the law be avoided. Perhaps the most striking case in the modern world is the NCAA. NCAA-sponsored competitions such as the basketball championship March Madness generate billions of dollars of revenue in the form of tickets, broadcast rights, and merchandising—and yet the players are paid nothing. This, however, is an exception to the general rule that wherever a sport generates revenue the players will end up winning a significant share.

How big a share varies in time and place. Back in 1953 the professional major league clubs paid an average of under 25 percent of their total revenue to the players in the form of salaries. Today the clubs pay about 60 percent of their revenue in salaries. A similar pattern can be seen in English league football. During the 1950s the professional clubs paid out 35–40 percent of their revenue to players, and by the end of the 1990s the figure was closer to 60 percent. Until the 1960s the most prestigious tennis tournaments, such as Wimbledon and Forest Hills, were open only to amateurs. Amateur status meant that the organizers of these tournaments retained all of the revenue (often using the money to fund development of the game) while the exclusion of professionals limited their status and therefore their earnings potential. Yet even in a sport like golf, where professionals were active and accepted in "open" tournaments, the prize funds remained relatively small until the 1950s.

The increasing share of revenue paid to players reflects their increasing bargaining power. In the major leagues player unions became active in the 1960s and threatened to strike unless their demands were met. In baseball the willingness of the players to carry out this threat (the first work stoppage in MLB occurred in 1972, and since then there have been a further seven) forced owners to make significant concessions. In 1961 the Professional Footballer's Association in England came within hours of a strike, called to oppose the maximum wage rule that limited a player's salary to £20 per week. Realizing that the players were prepared to carry out their threat, the owners backed down and the maximum wage was abolished (and within one year players' salaries increased from 40 percent to 50 percent of total club revenue). Similar militancy can be found in the actions of players in the non-team sports. For example, in 1973 the top professional tennis players boycotted Wimbledon as part of their campaign to secure greater control over the game through the Association of Tennis Players (ATP).

Since a game cannot be played without the players, and fans are prepared to pay the most in order to see the top players, one is led to wonder why players did not learn to flex their financial muscles before the 1960s. Some historians have attributed increasing militancy to the climate of the times and the greater emphasis on the rights of workers. In earlier times trade unions often faced political opposition from government and the judiciary, limiting their ability to organize effective opposition to "management."

But there was more than player power in the air in the 1950s. The advent of television transformed the economics of sport by dramatically expanding the audience for major events and increasing the amount of revenue they can generate. It is not the increasing share of revenue that has produced the dramatic increases in player rewards. The average player in MLB earned $17,000 per year in 1953, and is today paid around $2.5 million. Allowing for the impact of inflation, thanks to which you would need around $140,000 today to have a purchasing power equivalent to $17,000 in 1953, average salaries have risen nearly eighteenfold in today's money (that is, from $140,000 to $2.5 million). The players' share has risen from 20 percent to 60 percent of total revenue, so their cut of the cake has increased threefold. The bulk of their salary increases, therefore, have come from the growth in the size of the cake. Almost all of this increase can be attributed to increased media exposure, largely in the form of TV.

The dramatic increase in the earnings of sportsmen has prompted much public discussion. It is common to hear people say that a player cannot possibly be worth the salary he is being paid. Disgusted fans often compare players' salaries to those earned by nurses and firefighters. Moreover, most people consider it a privilege to play at the very highest level of sport, with all the public adulation that this brings. "I would do it for nothing," so the argument goes. "Why do they need to be paid such huge salaries?" And indeed, most top sportsmen say themselves that the money has very little to do with their motivation, suggesting that they would play just as well if they weren't paid.

To understand the relevance of these arguments, we need first to consider the function of wage payments in general. According to Karl Marx, in a utopian society a person would participate on the principle "From each according to his ability, to each according to his need." Thus there would be no connection between the resources allocated to people and their contribution to society. Setting aside the difficulty of determining exactly how much a person needs, the problem with this utopian vision is how to use people's abilities optimally. Market economies use wage payments to solve the problem in two ways; first, they are a motivator, rewarding the successful completion of tasks with additional resources; second, and perhaps more subtly, they match workers to jobs, making it more likely that a particular set of skills is employed where it is valued most highly.

On the face of it, it does not sound likely that money is a significant source of motivation in professional sports. If the salaries of professionals have risen nearly twentyfold, should we expect that sports stars try harder today? Certainly it would be nonsense to suggest that they are trying twenty times harder. However, there have been marginal effects on motivation. The biggest impact on performance in the last fifty years has come from improved training methods. Athletes are fitter than they ever were in the past, and some of this increased fitness results from a reduction in alcohol consumption. In the 1950s and 1960s star athletes sometimes drank heavily before games, even competed under the influence of alcohol. As players' salaries have risen, the threat of disciplinary action has curbed alcohol consumption, and while players still indulge in drinking and recreational drugs, they do so far less often than in the past. In this sense at least, money has motivated performance. It may have acted as a motivator in more negative ways as well. Some would say that there was more fair play and sportsmanship when salaries were low and differences in pay small. When the difference between winning and losing is worth millions of dollars, fair play can be costly. The use of performance-enhancing drugs in modern sports also reflects the increasing value attached to winning.

Increasing financial rewards for athletic talent have also motivated more and more young people to pursue an athletic career. Little boys have always wanted to be baseball or soccer stars, but at the same time adult voices have warned that there was little money in it, given the long odds of success. Today such warnings carry less weight even though the probability of becoming a sports star is literally one out of millions. Leaders of the African American community in the United States have lamented the tendency of young African Americans to neglect their studies in favor of athletics.

While these motivations act on the person, their overall effect has been to increase the supply of athletic talent. In the past many people with the ability to play sport at the highest level chose to pursue other activities. Today it is less likely that anyone with the ability to play at the highest level will fail to do so. Whether or not this is a good thing for society depends on the alternative careers that athletes might follow. In chapter 2 we mentioned Roger Bannister, who in 1954 became the first to run a mile in under four minutes. While in training as a miler Bannister was also a medical student, something that limited his training. However, he subsequently became a distinguished neurologist. Nowadays it seems unlikely that someone could pursue a twin career track in that way, and by the time an athletic career is over, it is probably too late to complete a medical degree. In other words, the financial reward to modern sports deprives society of talented people who would contribute through alternative careers in later life. The effect on society is probably small in practice, given the relatively small number of people who reach the highest level in sports. More significant may be the numbers of high school students who neglect their studies in the teenage years and fail to develop alternative skills. At the very least, the supply of disappointed young athletes has increased over the years.

This brings us to the question of whether athletes are paid too much relative to other professions. We could certainly increase the supply of nurses and firefighters if we offered an annual salary of $1 million or more. In fact, if the top five nurses and firefighters were paid $1 million, this would presumably lead to a huge increase in the number of young people aspiring to such careers. By the same token, there is little evidence that there is an inadequate supply of neurosurgeons to society, largely because a neurosurgeon can expect to earn hundreds of thousands of dollars per year, and so the medical schools are full of aspiring students. The truth about nurses and firefighters is that even at their relatively low wages a reasonably plentiful supply of people enters these professions (in developed countries shortages are usually dealt with by allowing immigration, often from low-income countries; shortages, if they exist, are mainly concentrated in regions where the pay on offer is extremely low). From an economic perspective, the salary structure in developed nations fulfills its role—ensuring an adequate supply of people for the jobs required.

The fact that athletes in the most popular sports are paid so much reflects the value that we as consumers place upon their services. Every dedicated Yankees fan drives up the price paid to acquire the top baseball players; every buyer of merchandise sold by Real Madrid increases the pay of the top soccer stars. Sometimes, ironically, the fans who complain most about the salaries of stars are precisely those whose intense support of their team drives up the players' wages. Similarly, the demand on the part of fans to get tickets to see Roger Federer or Tiger Woods increases their attractiveness and therefore increases the amount that organizers, sponsors, and broadcasters are willing to pay to secure their participation in an event.

Fans sometimes complain that the high wages paid to their team cause high ticket prices, although economic logic suggests that this is not the case. According to the economic argument, it is the demand of the fans themselves that causes high ticket prices, and even if players were paid nothing, the team owners would still charge high prices in order to make the biggest possible profits. In reality, however, teams compete for players, and do indeed raise prices when they secure the services of a top star, in the expectation that fans will be willing to pay more to see a more successful team.

In an economic sense this is simply a manifestation of the laws of supply and demand. By its nature athletic talent is scarce. While it is in great demand, it is in short supply. If players were paid the same as nurses, every small-town team would be bidding for the services of Alex Rodriguez or Cristiano Ronaldo. But they have been priced out of those markets. In reality only a small number of teams can afford these players, those with hordes of supporters whose ticket purchases can fund astronomic wages. The market is very good at ensuring that scarce resources are allocated to those who are willing to pay the most.

The trouble with this rational economic analysis is that it says nothing of fairness. While most people feel that it is fair to pay a neurologist millions of dollars in exchange for years of dedicated study and a capacity to save human lives, most people also feel that it is unfair to pay so much to people whose talent is largely a gift, to do something that many other people would gladly do for nothing, and which, at the end of the day, is not going to save lives. Some of this resentment is purely envy, and some of it is simply a misperception of the degree of skill (and training) involved in performing at the highest levels. Top athletes enjoy the prestige that they do because they are capable of doing things that the rest of us cannot, no matter how much we practice. Envy and ignorance aside, however, most of us recognize values that are distinct from the values of the market, and we become uncomfortable when economic values deviate too far from these values. Nurses help to save lives—they are valuable—whatever their market wage rate, and sports are just a game, however much we care about the result.

To take a different example, after Hurricane Katrina in 2005 many suppliers of gasoline in affected areas raised their prices, reflecting the shortage caused by the widespread disruption of supply. To an economist this was just the operation of supply and demand, while to most other citizens it was price gouging. To an economist, rising prices ensure that gas goes to those who value it most, distributing a scarce resource where it is most needed while also creating an incentive for suppliers to bring more gas to the market (to share in the profit). To most other people, including Congress, higher gas prices came across as unscrupulous and unfair.

The point here is that economists advocate supply and demand as a way to allocate resources because markets are efficient. When quizzed about fairness, they respond that it can be dealt with in other ways—for example, by taxes and subsidies. A typical economist's argument would be that if a majority of citizens agreed that fairness is important, they would elect a government to distribute resources equally among citizens, and the fact that they do not shows that people are quite content with inequality. This is, perhaps, to underestimate the subtlety of the electorate. It is not inconsistent to find the allocation produced by the market unfair while refusing to vote for those who promise to rectify the unfairness by taking from the rich to give to the poor. History is replete with examples of unscrupulous politicians who want unlimited powers to make the world a fairer place, only to leave everyone worse off than before. In fact, the world we live in is unfair, but a world in which resources were allocated by politicians and their friends might be even more unfair. This seems to summarize the position taken by many sports fans today: the wages paid to players are outrageous, but there are no obvious ways to bring them down.

Team owners in the United States and the national federations that govern European sports have taken advantage of the fans' aversion to high player salaries to defend the restrictions they have imposed on the labor market. The reserve rule in baseball and the transfer system in soccer held down the wages of players by preventing teams from competing for the best players, but no one ever argued that the system deprived baseball or soccer of the best talent. In effect, the clubs agreed to hold down wages to the lowest level consistent with attracting players. The maximum wage system in English soccer seems to have tested the limits of this theory—when it was abolished in 1961, the maximum of £20 per week compared unfavorably with the wages earned by skilled manual laborers. Yet there was little indication that young stars were abandoning soccer to work in factories.

In response to players' demand that they be given freedom to move between teams, owners and administrators argued that freedom of movement would simply increase wages and deprive the clubs of money to invest in facilities and better teams, harming the interests of fans. It is questionable whether in reality teams do invest more when wages are low. From the perspective of profit maximization, investment in the team and in the facilities is a matter of marginal revenue and marginal cost—whether the extra revenue from investment outweighs the cost. For example, it is worth building extra seats if enough extra fans are prepared to pay for the seats over the life of the investment, and this calculation is independent of the wages paid to the players themselves. It was sometimes argued that low wages were necessary so that clubs could accumulate enough profit to cover the cost of construction, but in fact such internal financing was not really necessary—if the investment produced a return, then it would be possible to borrow from banks rather than rely on internally generated funds. In the case where the club directors were not acting so as to maximize profit, but instead chose to spend all the revenue they received, low wages would indeed allow teams to spend more on players, but in this situation teams tended to engage in stockpiling—hiring more players than were strictly necessary. In European leagues where roster limits have never existed, the number of professional soccer players has fallen over time as player wages have risen and teams have concentrated their resources. There is certainly no evidence that not-for-profit teams spent more on facilities when wages were low; indeed, the long neglect of stadium facilities in Europe endured throughout the period when wages were held down, and only in recent years, when wages have risen, has investment increased.

Regardless of whether the argument had any economic validity, the claim that holding down wages was in the best interests of the sport resonated with the general public, who found little sympathy with the idea that sports stars were underpaid. And when player militancy or (as in Europe) the legal requirement to allow free movement of labor forced up player wages, it was frequently the players who were seen as the villains of the piece. The principal economic effect of competition for players (other than rising wages) appears to be that the team that places the greatest economic value on a player is the one that succeeds in employing him. To most fans this is a dubious benefit, since few of them believe that economic might should be the arbitrator of sporting outcomes. In America the fans have come to view negotiations over wages between players and their employers as a dispute between millionaires and billionaires, neither of whom they can empathize with. In Europe, where many clubs are financed by subscriptions paid by ordinary members, and where most clubs are in a precarious financial position, the players are often accused of endangering the future of their club through their greed. The phenomenon of the player's agent in Europe and the United States is relatively recent. Players appoint agents to work out their financial deals, which makes a lot of sense given that their employers are well versed in business practices. For many, however, the player and his agent have come to be seen as vampires feeding off the lifeblood of the sport, an image that the clubs and the governing bodies have done much to promote.

The difference between the wages paid to players and the minimum that they would need to be paid to persuade them to play is called "economic rent." The concept of rent was first explored in relation to land by the economists Adam Smith and David Ricardo two hundred years ago. Ricardo noticed that agricultural products sold at the same price regardless of the productivity of the land on which they were grown, implying that the profits on some land (that which is most productive) are greater than on other land. The increasing demand for food meant that less productive land was brought under cultivation, up to the point where the supply of food equaled demand. The greater the demand for food, the greater the economic rents accruing to the more productive land. These economic rents in themselves serve no direct economic purpose, since the land would remain under cultivation as long as the cost of growing crops was covered. Moreover, since the land is held mainly by the wealthy landowner class, many economists have argued that landowners should be heavily taxed in order to redistribute the economic rent. This argument has sometimes been advanced in relation to player salaries, although it seems unlikely that a special sports star tax would ever be considered viable.

Economists have found that professional sport is well suited for conducting research on the operation of labor markets. In most labor markets it is possible to observe information about the wage payments, but in general very little is known about the characteristics of employees, and confidentiality limits the opportunity to develop detailed databases. Even if such data is available, little is usually known about the precise performance of each worker and their contribution to total production. Finally, it is seldom possible to compare the performance of a given worker in different firms. In sports all of this data is often available. Economists can research questions such as the impact of employers' power on wages (for example, by analyzing the impact of the reserve rule) or the existence of discrimination by employers (by comparing workers who show similar performance but are from different races or ethnic groups).

In the 1970s Gerald Scully showed that it is possible to estimate the economic contribution of a baseball player to his team, thanks to data generated by baseball statisticians. His approach involved two sets of calculations. First he estimated the value of an additional win to each team in terms of extra revenue, and then he estimated the contribution of different performance measures, such as runs scored and runs batted in (RBI), to the production of wins. The combination of these two measures then provides an estimate of the financial contribution of a player to his club in a season. Scully identified these estimates with what economists call the marginal revenue product—the extra revenue that a small improvement in individual performance would produce for the team. In a competitive market the wages of players would be bid up to this level—otherwise another team would be able to hire the player and generate additional profits. What Scully showed was that in the days before free agency wages were far below marginal revenue product—reflecting the fact that the reserve clause held wages down. Competition for the services of players following the abolition of the reserve clause and the advent of free agency in 1976 caused the salaries of baseball players to rise rapidly toward their marginal product.

In fact, what happened is a nice illustration of markets in operation. Free agency only applied to six-year veterans, meaning that after six years a player could sell his services to the highest bidder, but players with fewer years of service were still subject to the reserve clause. Veterans are in relatively scarce supply, since each season only fifty or so players reach the six-year mark (although some older veterans will also come back onto the market as their free agency contract expires). There is a lot of variation in these salaries as clubs compete for the best free agents, and even some evidence that teams overbid, meaning that a player can be paid significantly more than his marginal revenue product. Players with less than six years service but more than three years are eligible for salary arbitration, meaning that they can require an independent panel to determine what a fair salary would be, rather than accepting the offer of the employer. Estimates showed that these players were closer to being paid their marginal revenue product than they had been in the past, although their salaries were still below this mark. Rookies, with little or no bargaining power, are generally estimated to be furthest away from earning what their productivity says they are worth.

It is one thing to say that players *as a whole* are paid more or less than they are worth. But Scully's model also implies that *each individual* player will be paid in proportion to the value that they bring to a team. Based on traditional baseball statistics such as RBIs, Scully's model implies that the market for players is efficient, in the same sense that the stock market is efficient. This doesn't mean that every share on the stock market with the same price will produce the same returns to an investor, or that each player with the same salary will be equally productive on the field. Rather, it means stocks or players commanding *higher* prices should on average be expected to perform better, and that if two players or stocks have the *same* price it should be impossible to predict which stock or which player will underperform or overperform. This is fine, so long as the right measures of performance are used.

On the stock market analysts try to use indicators such as accounting data to predict which stocks will be successful, but market efficiency means that any indicator that can help predict the future gets instantly written into the share price, and so ends up being no more use than the share price itself as an indicator of future value. To see how this works, imagine a company announces that its profits have risen 20 percent, when previously analysts had expected its profits to rise by 10 percent. As soon as the announcement is made, sellers of the shares increase their asking price, because the information has revealed some good news about the company's performance. Thus the information tells us something about the value of the shares, but that information is instantly incorporated in the price. The only way you could profit from the accounting information would be if you could get hold of the information before the seller, and that would probably require insider information.

It is not clear how reliably this process works in baseball or other sports. Baseball is especially interesting because it has such a plethora of performance statistics that can be used to value players. Generations of Americans have pored lovingly over baseball statistics, but the computer age has begun to influence baseball in the way that it has transformed stock market analysis. From the 1970s on a number of baseball fans have looked for new ways to measure player productivity, and found that many of the traditional measures, such as RBIs and stolen bases, can be remarkably poor indicators of productivity. Many of these people organized around the Society for American Baseball Research (SABR) and became known as sabermetricians. Bill James has been the leading proponent of the proposition that (*a*) traditional statistical measures may be poor indicators of performance and (*b*) intelligently constructed measures can help identify ways to improve performance.

The baseball establishment has been slow to adopt statistical techniques, despite their obvious potential. One simple reason is that baseball is not like the stock market, where anyone can buy or sell stock that is inappropriately valued and make a profit. Rather, baseball is run by thirty owners who have been willing to act collusively in the past. Many people have condemned the attitude of owners and general managers as being driven by their stubbornness and stupidity, but there is a more subtle explanation. Innovation typically increases costs, and therefore cartels usually suppress innovation unless they face competition from the outside. If we contrast this situation with the world of soccer, where teams face more intense competition because of the institution of promotion and relegation, we also find a much closer correlation between players' salaries and team performance, suggesting that owners are seeking the best measures of productivity and applying them in their purchasing decisions.

Even in baseball there are signs that the owners are starting to apply the information that statistical methods and computers can supply. *Moneyball*, the best-selling analysis of Billy Beane's strategy for improving the performance of the Oakland Athletics, explains how the application of better information was able to improve the productivity of a team without spending any more money. What Beane discovered was that on-base percentage was being undervalued by the other teams—they tended to value hits but not fully appreciate the contribution from being walked. Being walked, however, is often a consequence of the batter's ability. Beane went after players that looked relatively poor by conventional statistics but had abnormally high on-base percentages. The strategy paid off by rewarding Oakland with a better team performance than would have been achieved by another team spending the same amount of money on players. In effect, this is little different from the exploitation of any trading opportunity in the market. Subsequent research has shown that this market opportunity has since disappeared, as other teams have learned to recognize the value of on-base percentage, just as we would expect in the stock market if a new source of information on the value of shares were found.

Models such as Scully's and its successors, by relating individual contributions to economic returns and then comparing economic returns to the wages paid to the player, illustrate the extent to which the market operates efficiently, matching players to teams where their contribution is most highly valued. This observation has also generated research on economic discrimination, by enabling researchers to test whether characteristics such as race have an independent effect on the wages earned by players. Again, this kind of research is difficult to pursue in other labor markets since individual productivity data is generally hard to come by. Researchers have even been able to test whether salary differences are attributable to the fans or the owners, by testing whether the performance of players of equal ability but different race had different impacts on the attendance at ballparks. In general this literature has shown that discrimination against black players in North America does exist, in the sense that they tend to be paid less than white players of equal ability. Some of this difference is attributable to bias on the part of fans, as was shown in a study that looked at the trading prices of baseball cards, which found that the cards of black players traded for less (after accounting for ability). Some of the difference is also attributable to owners.

Similar evidence of discrimination has been found in ice hockey in Canada, where Francophone Canadians have often found it difficult to find employment with Anglophone Canadian teams. There is less research on these issues in European soccer, largely because data on individual salaries is almost impossible to find. Some studies have suggested evidence of discrimination in English soccer, but the picture is complicated by the international nature of the player market. There is evidence from Italy, for example, that players from Argentina and Brazil are overpaid relative to their abilities. This can be explained by the entertainment value associated with the distinctive style of play found in those countries—it may not always win games, but it is pretty to watch, and the fans value this aspect of the South American style.

In recent years researchers have become more ambitious, and have attempted to test more sophisticated labor market theories using sporting data. There is a large sociological literature on motivation, which tends to focus on notions of equity and the matching of rewards to expectations in the labor market. The idea of "a fair day's work for a fair day's pay" resonates powerfully with most employees, and much of what goes on in pay bargaining is about establishing norms of fairness. These can vary widely depending on the workers and the context, so that it becomes difficult to establish what it is that makes one team of workers more motivated than another. There is also little doubt that what people will do in a job depends to a significant degree on what they believe they are capable of achieving and whether the goals they have been set are reasonable. Once again, personality plays a significant role in determining what might be considered reasonable. It is frequently noted in sports that a given group of players will perform better for one coach than another. On this observation is built a huge literature on motivation in sports, much of which is aimed at crossing over into more general management practice. However, there are two important drawbacks with this approach.

The first problem is that it is not clear that what works in sports will work in other fields of economic activity. Managing sports stars may have something in common with managing movie stars, but probably has little to do with managing autoworkers, and most of the leading sports managers are wise enough to recognize this. They tend to talk in general terms about lessons in motivation rather than the application of specific training techniques. In many cases it may be that the specific training techniques are the source of success, not the motivational talks.

Second, even a brief reading of studies of motivation shows that successful coaches employ different methods—some aggressive, some gentle, some strict, some permissive, some close and personal, some distant and hierarchical. Given that all of these methods have achieved success at some time or other, it seems unlikely that there is any simple formula. What most famous coaches have in common is charisma—something that in general cannot be learned but is a prerequisite for success. In the film *Being There* Peter Sellers plays a gardener whose simplistic utterances are interpreted as profound insight, and the film ends with him on the verge of becoming a candidate for the U.S. presidency, despite having no relevant knowledge. One aspect of this satire is its mockery of our desire to find an explanation for things where there is none. Brian Clough, whose ability to turn players rejected by big teams into major stars is unparalleled in the history of soccer, made the following observation in his autobiography: "They tell me people have always wondered how I did it. That fellow professionals and public alike have been fascinated and puzzled and intrigued by the Clough managerial methods and technique and would love to know my secret. I've got news for all of them—so would I." At the turn of the twentieth century Frederick Winslow Taylor talked of "scientific management," in which every contribution to productivity could be measured and controlled. But people are not robots, and despite intensive research into the theory of motivation, there is still little consensus on what works and what does not.

The economic theory of motivation is a simple one. A person will contribute effort in any given situation up to the point where the marginal benefit equals the marginal cost. Suppose an employer (generally known as the "principal" in economics) wants an employee (or "agent") to carry out some task. According to theory it is sufficient to offer compensation that is large enough to ensure that doing the job is more profitable for the agent than not doing the job. This rule is called the "participation constraint." In sports the athletes are paid well in excess of what is required by the participation constraint. In addition to the participation constraint, however, there is also the "incentive compatibility constraint." This states that to get the job done the agent must prefer to carry out the task rather than pretend to do it, or underperform in some other way. Incentive compatibility is quite easy to satisfy in a world where the task to be done is clearly defined. In such a world the principal makes a simple offer to the agent: do the job to my satisfaction in return for a fixed payment, or you will get nothing. Consider, for example, a homeowner who wants to sell property and sets a minimum price—the ideal contract with a realtor in this situation is the promise of a fixed fee if the house is sold and zero otherwise. Equivalently, the homeowner might sell the house to the realtor for the minimum price, leaving the realtor with the job of selling it.

Achieving incentive compatibility in this way has two drawbacks. First, the realtor would need to have enough wealth to finance the transaction. This system does work for some kinds of transaction, but in most cases it is not feasible. The factory owner cannot sell the factory to the employees as a way of ensuring that they finish a job. Nowadays, of course, owners could sell the team to the players, given their wealth. In a sense this is what has happened in professional tennis and golf, where the players' organization has taken an increasing role in the management of the tour. The second drawback is that tying an agent's rewards to the completion of the job means that the employee bears all the risk, and risk bearing can be extremely costly. Most people buy insurance precisely because they do not like to bear risk. Taking financial responsibility for a business transaction is risky because the outcome depends not only on the effort of the worker but also on the contribution of other factors, many of which are beyond the control of the employee. The value of a house depends on the state of the market, the quality of a product often depends on the inputs of hundreds of people, and the outcome of a sports tournament depends on a whole host of factors beyond the control of the athlete—in other words, plain luck. That is, the output of an employee depends on skill, effort, and multiple factors outside the control of the employee.

The alternative to making rewards depend on the outcome is to make rewards depend on contributions made by the employee—ability and effort. This again is straightforward if ability and effort are easily defined and measured, but in general they are not. What principals know is that better outcomes are more likely when employees contribute more effort, and they design reward schemes accordingly. Most contracts involve some element of fixed payment, as a kind of insurance for the employee against the risk of bad outcomes, plus a variable bonus that depends on the outcome of the activity. In some professions the incentive element is large; examples include salesmen working on commission or investment bankers whose income is mostly derived from their annual bonus. In most cases, however, employees face relatively low-powered incentive schemes—nurses and university professors are paid more or less the same amount no matter how well or how poorly they perform.

Because low-powered incentive schemes do not work well in terms of incentive compatibility (workers have limited financial incentives to supply effort), there has been much research on ways to sharpen incentives. In recent years there has been increasing focus on comparing the performance of employees—compiling league tables of research output in universities or recovery rates in hospitals. Those whose performance is near the top end of the table are offered additional rewards, while those near the bottom are monitored more closely. The idea behind these schemes is that when individual performance is hard to measure and reward, relative performance can help to sharpen incentives.

There has been considerable interest in the application of such ideas to sporting contests, since on the face of it these are classic examples of relative performance schemes; rewards in sports are almost entirely dependent on relative performance. Thus the gold medal goes to the sprinter who breaks the tape, regardless of the speed. In some sports the athletes take advantage of this fact to conserve effort—as in the case of cycling races where the competitors move at the slowest speed possible until the very end of the race, when they suddenly sprint for the finish line. There is, however, a significant difference between sports and other forms of labor. In sports, the outcome of the contest is the reason for working in the first place, the end in itself. In most employment situations, creating artificial contests is a means to an end, namely the enhancement of overall productivity.

As the example of the cyclists suggests, creating contests for incentive purposes is not entirely satisfactory. Rather than trying to perform to the best of one's ability the objective is to be slightly better than someone else. This can lead to underperformance and even sabotage, since the inferior performance of rivals also increases your probability of being rated highly. Incentives based on relative performance can have a role to play when it is difficult to measure individual productivity. It is generally much more reliable to base rewards on individual performance where that information is available. This is one reason why relative performance incentives are seldom used in team sports. While players may receive bonuses for winning, much of what a player is paid is independent of their performance during the life of the contract. However, there are many reasons to think it unlikely that players take advantage of this by underperforming. First, performance during a game and in training is easily observed. Players who are not delivering during a game are particularly noticeable and liable to experience pressure from fans and coaches alike to increase their effort. Second, there are many forms of sanction available for underperforming players: dropping them from the team, requiring them to undertake additional training, and so on. Third, the longer-term costs of underperforming are huge; these include the threat that the contract will not be renewed and the loss of endorsement income, this latter source of income being more important than salary for many players. The idea that players can "get away" with shirking on the job seems unlikely, and therefore incentive schemes designed to limit such shirking are not likely to be important.

Whether athletes ever shirk is an interesting question. The commitment required to become a top athlete is so great and the rewards so huge that it seems hard to imagine it ever happens. However, shirking can be broadly defined. Suppose the coach assigns a task to a player as part of the team's defensive plan, but the player deviates from the assigned task—this is a form of shirking that may arise out of the player's pursuit of personal glory or simply a failure to recognize the importance of the plan to the team. Such things do happen. Overcoming this kind of shirking is hard since coaches seldom want to remove all autonomy from the players, for sometimes the unexpected action wins the game. Off the field, athletes can shirk in other ways. A common problem is the failure to stay fit, through lack of application in the gym or through consumption of alcohol or recreational drugs. A different kind of shirking is overstating injuries. Because of the rules of the salary cap in the NFL, some teams have increased the share of total wages paid in the form of signing bonuses. One study found that these teams underperformed on the field, suggesting that large upfront payments had diminished players' incentives. Given the likelihood of injury in the NFL, it would make sense for a player already guaranteed a large salary to conserve his health until near the end of his contract, when he might again hope to be hired for a large signing bonus.

But by and large, shirking in top professional sports is today a marginal issue because the rewards for making effort are so large. It was not always so. In the days when top athletes were paid relatively little and the rewards from winning were not significant, there was an incentive for athletes to distort outcomes for personal gain. Match fixing is a phenomenon largely associated with gambling, although it can also occur when someone places a very high value on the outcome for other reasons, such as national pride (stories of match fixing in the soccer World Cup abound). Match fixing is a particular kind of bias, which involves financial compensation to produce a given result, not to be confused with other kinds of bias such as that uncovered in sumo by Steven Levitt (referred to at the beginning of chapter 2) or racial discrimination. Recent research has found evidence of biases in the decision making in professional baseball, basketball, and soccer.

Match fixing in leagues can occur when there are large financial inequalities between the teams. In soccer big clubs have sometimes valued success so much that they have been willing to pay to win championships or avoid relegation. In 2006 Juventus, one of the most successful clubs in the history of Italian soccer, was relegated to Serie B (the second level) for the first time in their history after being found guilty of influencing the choice of referees to their advantage.

There is a relatively straightforward economic relationship between match fixing and gambling. The fixer can make money by betting on an unlikely outcome and then making sure that it comes to pass. A referee in Germany in 2005 fixed a game between Paderborn, a small team, and Hamburg, a big team, so that the former won. The case came to light because of the extraordinary actions that the referee had to take to create the result— sending off a player who had done nothing wrong and awarding a phantom penalty. In this way the gambler made a large profit from the exceptional result, more than enough to cover the payoff to the referee.

Most sports can cite examples of fixing games. Perhaps the most famous is that of "Shoeless Joe" Jackson and the 1919 Black Sox scandal. Jackson, who held the second highest lifetime batting average in baseball (.354), was earning a mere $6,000 a year (equivalent to about $76,000 in today's money). Even by the standards of the day, Charles Comiskey, the owner of the White Sox, was a notoriously mean employer. Whether Jackson was party to the fix or not, there is no doubt that all of the players had an adequate financial incentive to take part in it. In 1965 ten English soccer players were jailed for conspiracy to defraud by fixing the outcome of matches on which they had placed bets. Most of the games were played in the early 1960s, when the average footballer earned less than £20 per week. Points shaving scandals (points shaving generally means not trying to lose, but not trying to win by as wide a margin as expected, in order to make a profit from spread betting) seem to be endemic in college basketball, where the players are not paid, and date back at least to the 1950s (a recent film dealt with a City College of New York scandal in 1951). Some of the worst betting scandals occurred in the supposedly gentlemanly game of cricket. At the end of the 1990s it was discovered that the captains of most of the principal cricketing nations had been engaged in match fixing in one form or another. The captain of South Africa was dismissed from his job (and several years later died mysteriously in a plane crash). One contributory factor recognized by the cricket authorities was the relatively low pay of the players.

In any case of match fixing, the fundamental elements of supply and demand must balance. From the point of view of the "buyer," fixing matches is generally important only when there is great interest in the sport and a significant return is to be made by controlling the outcome, usually through gambling. The potential match fixer must be able to significantly influence the outcome, so that in general only the stars are likely to be approached. On the "selling" side, the players must balance the reward from fixing against the potential cost of being caught. This cost is the probability of being caught multiplied by the penalty for fixing. In almost all sports the most draconian penalty available to authorities is deprivation of sporting income by exclusion from participation in the sport. Raising salaries of the top players is therefore a way of raising the penalty for cheating. Moreover, raising salaries also diminishes the attractiveness of illicit income. To put it simply, a player paid $100,000 a year would find a bribe of $100,000 much more attractive than the same player earning $1,000,000 a year. High salaries in sports do not eliminate all cheating, and may not even eliminate match fixing, but they do make it much less likely. Match fixing for gambling purposes today tends to be associated either with the match officials (who tend to be paid relatively little), or with sports where the athlete's pay is low (due to limited interest from anyone other than gamblers, or where the amateur code forbids payment).

Many people argue that the problem today is not that athletes have insufficient incentives to make effort, but that their efforts go beyond the bounds of what is acceptable. "Cheating to win," rather than "cheating to lose," is likely to occur when there are large differences between the rewards for different levels of success. When the prize for coming in first dwarfs the prizes for coming in second or third, participants become desperate to use every means possible to win. In addition to sabotage, the use of performance-enhancing drugs is largely a consequence of the winner-take-all reward system that is characteristic of professional sports.

The predominant concern today is cheating through taking illicit substances—although there are other forms. For example, in the world of chess there have long been accusations of secret messages being sent, hypnotism, and other dark arts. Spying on rivals' tactics has become a problem in a number of sports, most notably during the recent "Spygate" scandal in American football, where the dominant New England team took illicit videos of rivals' practice sessions (a similar scandal affected Rugby Union).

Athletes have always taken substances that they thought would enhance their performance, and in retrospect many of these seem silly. For example, when official testing was introduced in the 1968 Olympics, the Swedish pentathlete Hans-Gunnar Liljenwall was disqualified for using alcohol, which would hardly be considered a performance-enhancing substance today. Nonetheless, the development of synthetic drugs, which can affect mental states and bodily development, have posed increasing concerns from the 1930s onward. The most problematic substances have been steroids, which help athletes to build muscle and compete well beyond the levels possible without these substances. Abuse seems nearly universal in sport, whether it be to build stamina (cycling), power (weight lifting, baseball), or speed (sprints). The former Communist regime in East Germany, which won an alarming number of Olympic medals during the Cold War, was one of the prime movers in the culture of doping. However, the thirst for fame and success has been equally powerful in the capitalist world. Athletes seem to be pressurized from a very early age by coaches, eager to see their protégés succeed, and even by fellow athletes, perhaps seeking to assuage their own sense of guilt. All this is despite the evidence that persistent abuse can lead to medical problems and even an early death.

Although the doping problem in sport has been recognized for many decades, it was not until 1999 that the IOC set up WADA, the World Anti-Doping Agency, to coordinate national efforts to control drug abuse and to impose common limits. National sporting federations are encouraged to conduct random drug tests for banned substances, and the standard penalties on being found guilty of an abuse are a two-year ban for the first instance and a lifetime ban for the second. While doping is believed to be widespread, very few are caught—only around one-quarter of 1 percent of those tested. It seems likely that those trying to police the illegal use of substances are always outnumbered and one step behind the developers. Moreover, the usefulness of taking substances such as steroids is often greatest during training rather than during competition itself, making it hard to track down exactly when the abuse takes place. Even when athletes are caught, they are often able to get decisions overturned since taking samples and protecting them from contamination is often difficult.

The fundamental problem is that however much the organizers say they are determined to stamp out the illegal use of performance-enhancing drugs, the value of the competitive advantage from taking them is greater than the risk of being caught. Doping is likely to be a bigger problem in the big-money sports, and seldom a problem in sports with limited following, and limited financial returns. But even some sports with lesser financial rewards are subject to cheating problems, for example, weightlifting and chess; if the costs of competing are high enough (years of painful or exhausting preparation) and the opportunities to win are limited, the incentive to cheat also increases. Some argue that there is nothing wrong with consenting adults taking such substances as long as they understand the risks, and that legalizing drugs would at least have the benefit of leveling the playing field. While there is some merit in the argument, the concern is that if drug taking were legalized, it would reach further down into school athletics departments, so that even young children would take them, something that most people find unacceptable. From an economic perspective the monitoring of drug taking is like a tax on cigarettes—it does not eliminate smoking but it does reduce the number of smokers. The worry is that technological advances are making drugs cheaper and harder to detect. New forms of abuse such as gene therapies are now within the financial reach of athletes. The result is that monitoring is becoming more and more worthless. In every other walk of life, effort increases when the returns to effort increase. It would be perverse to expect sport and doping to be any different.

Five

SPORTS AND BROADCASTING

Broadcasting has transformed the nature of spectator sport. Just as recording technologies have enhanced the earning power of pop stars, so broadcasting has enabled the top athletes to reach a global audience. This has been the prime motivator behind the explosion of salaries at the top end of the talent distribution, but has also narrowed the demand for the less talented. In the 1930s minor league baseball in the United States and second-division soccer in England drew huge audiences. Once TV made the top teams available for all, demand for the second tier of competition fell.

Originally the organizers of sports were wary of TV, fearing that attendance would fall as many people stayed home to watch, and others would get bored with watching games played in empty stadiums. However, in most sports it soon became apparent that broadcasting could enhance demand by showcasing the teams and drawing more supporters. To this day the principal ambition of minor sports is to obtain TV coverage, and they will often supply their games to broadcasters for free. TV transformed the relationships between clubs and leagues and between players and teams. TV enhanced the power of the big clubs and tended to weaken the power of smaller clubs. But TV also taught the big clubs the value of "league-think," as they call it in the NFL, meaning the benefit of collective decision-making to produce a coherent package for the broadcaster. TV also required players to band together to negotiate with their employers. When revenue was attendance-driven, each player's contribution could be directly measured in terms of the number of extra fans at the stadium that their performances produced. Once revenue was derived from league-wide TV contracts, each player became a joint contributor to the general revenue of the league, and the contribution of an individual player became harder to measure.

As an entertainment, sports create huge benefits for consumers measured by the amount of time devoted to thinking and talking about them. Without them many people would find their lives, not to mention their capacity to engage in conversation, significantly diminished. But sports clubs extract very little of the economic surplus they generate—largely because they cannot tax the discussions and arguments that their activities feed. Sports broadcasting has enabled the clubs to take a larger share of the surplus they generate, first through advertising on free-to-air TV, but increasingly through pay TV services. Improvements in technology are generating new ways to extract revenue from sports, including mobile phones and broadband Internet.

The restructuring of sport around TV has important implications for the way sports are organized. American football is a model of how a sport can be built around TV coverage, and it does not seem accidental that it has become the biggest revenue generator of any sports league in the world. More recently the highest level of soccer competition in Europe has been redesigned to create a product more attractive to TV audiences, and it is likely that pressure from TV companies will cause further changes to the structure of competition in the future.

From a technological point of view, probably the single greatest contributor to the birth of modern professional sports was the steam engine. Without the steam engine, it would have been unrealistic to transport athletes over long distances to engage in regular league competition. This was true even in a small country like Great Britain, where the greatest distance that most teams might have to travel would be three hundred miles; how much more true, therefore, was it in the United States, where distances can be counted in thousands of miles. Without the ability to draw together the best athletes it is unlikely that sports competitions could have attracted very large crowds. In other words, the commercial viability of modern professional sports depends on the ability to assemble teams of top athletes that can travel to the major urban centers to compete against each other.

However, once professional sport was established, people other than those able to attend in person wanted to know the outcome. For the last one hundred years it has been the development of broadcasting technologies that has dominated the development of modern sport. The earliest form of "broadcasting" was simply the newspaper. Henry Chadwick (1824–1908) is known as the "father of baseball" largely because of his efforts to spread interest in the game through the broadsheets (he was also a keen writer on cricket, and an advocate of soccer over football at the turn of the twentieth century). The institution of the "back pages" is a venerable one indeed.

It was the telegraph that first entered the market to compete with printed media, and in the 1890s the National League did a deal with Western Union to transmit results to bars and poolrooms. The advent of moving pictures at the turn of the century, however, did not make much of a difference. Unlike the telegraph, the movies lacked the immediacy that is the hallmark of the relationship between sport and broadcasting. The oldest proposition in sport is the "uncertainty-of-outcome hypothesis," discussed at length in chapters 2 and 3. Its most immediate application is to the value of a broadcast right. The Super Bowl and the World Cup final might be the most valuable minutes shown on television in a year, but one hour after the game has been played, 99 percent of the value of the right to show it has evaporated. Once the outcome is known, even fans who did not see it live place little value upon it. The value lies in not knowing what is going to happen next.

The first wave of the broadcasting revolution was the radio. By the end of World War I the possibility of wireless communication generated a new business and a new business model. In its original form broadcasting constituted what economists call a "public good." Economics uses this term in a narrow sense, to mean a product or service that is (*a*) nonexcludable (meaning that once it is supplied, there is no way to stop anyone from consuming it) and (*b*) nonrival in consumption (meaning consumption of the public good by one person does not prevent another person from consuming it). Quite clearly, most goods are not public goods. A glass of beer, for example, is both excludable (it can be sold to a consumer whose property right over the glass of beer is defensible in a court of law if need be) and rivalrous: if I drink it, then you cannot (and hence if I drink your beer you may indeed sue me). The business model for selling "private goods" is simple enough. You open a store and place them on the counter and people buy them for money.

The original radio broadcast signal was an example of a public good. Once the signal was transmitted, anyone with a wireless receiver could obtain the benefit of the broadcast program, regardless of whether they had paid anyone for the right to tune in. Moreover, the fact that one listener tuned in on one receiver made no difference to the ability of another listener to tune in on another receiver (or, if close enough, to hear the signal coming from the same device, as modern commuters know from their ability to listen to other peoples' MP3 players, however unwillingly!).

How to treat public goods is problematic for both public policy and business practice. From a public policy perspective, public goods may be highly desirable, but getting anyone to pay for them is difficult. The classic example is the lighthouse. Once the light shines upon the ocean, any ship that passes can benefit from the light, whether it agrees to pay the lighthouse owner or not. More subtly, it is not ideal to charge ships that pass, since they place no burden on the producer and exclude no one else from the light. If users of the light knew that they would be forced to pay a charge for it, they might even put off making a journey, even though their use of the light would not really cost anybody anything.[1] So not only is it difficult to get people to pay for public goods, it is not even clear that people should pay. However, if no one pays, then the service cannot be supplied in the first

---

[1] Economic theory is strongly opposed to the idea of stopping people from doing what they want to do when they impose no cost on anyone else. The root of this doctrine lies in the idea that the sum of human happiness will be greatest when all are free to do what they want, so long as they don't interfere in anyone else's right to do what he or she chooses.

place. In many cases the problem is solved by government stepping in to supply the public good out of taxpayers' money. Lighthouses are one example of government support, prompting the famous definition: "A lighthouse is a tall building on the shore maintained at public expense by the friend of a politician."

However, the new radio services demonstrated that there was a new and viable business model for the supply of public broadcast signals. By charging advertisers for the right to insert commercial breaks within broadcast programs, it was possible to finance the cost of acquiring broadcast equipment, erecting masts, and even subsidizing the acquisition of wireless receivers. No doubt the early broadcasters, enthused with the revolutionary implications of their new technology, imagined that the organizer of any activity that they chose to broadcast would be thankful for the honor bestowed upon them and roll out the red carpet. The baseball teams thought otherwise, and at once the question arose of how much would be paid, and to whom, for the right to broadcast a game on the newfangled radio.

There are basically four candidates for the ownership rights. The first is the owner of the stadium itself. The logic of this idea is the same as the logic of charging spectators. Spectators cannot see the game unless they gain access to the stadium, and the owner of the stadium has the right to deny access to the property, and will deny access unless a fee is paid for the right to enter. Of course, a broadcaster is more than a simple spectator, needing to bring equipment into the stadium and needing to take up some of the prime viewing space in order to provide the best possible commentary (and later, of course, video). Hence the broadcaster can be charged much more than the ordinary fan. Furthermore, broadcasters reach a bigger audience if they can cover the same events at fixed intervals (for example, weekly), creating what is sometimes called an "appointment to view," and thus are willing to pay a premium rather like a season ticket holder.

The second candidates are the owners of the teams playing the game. When the Rolling Stones play a concert, the stadium owner does not record the gig and sell it in competition with existing Rolling Stones products. One reason is that the Rolling Stones possess a copyright to the songs that they write, and they use this copyright to prohibit the resale or retransmission of recordings without their permission. Major leagues also rely on this right, and nowadays go to the length of making sure that this prohibition is repeated by the announcers during the broadcast of a game.

Usually the owner of the home team also owns the stadium, and hence there is no inherent conflict between stadium owners and team owners. However, the logic of copyright suggests that the owner of the visiting team can claim a share of ownership in the broadcast rights of games in which it participates. This problem is also dealt with in a way analogous to the treatment of revenue from ticket sales; there is a reciprocity implicit in a sports league, according to which the visiting team waives any financial claim over revenues generated from its road games in exchange for a similar waiver by rival teams in relation to its home games. The shared nature of the product sold to a broadcaster has brought home to many team owners the collective nature of their enterprise and so encouraged collective selling.

The third set of candidates is the players themselves. Players have long generated income from selling their endorsement of products. The ability to prevent others from using a performer's image without permission required the courts to create a new kind of right, usually referred to as publicity rights or image rights. But these rights potentially conflict with copyright, and in the 1980s the Major League Baseball Players' Association challenged the right of the clubs to sell broadcast rights as an infringement of the players' publicity rights. The owners claimed that the rights were implicit in the employment contract of the players, and that in general copyright goes to the employer who commissioned the "work," not the employees. In this case the union lost, with the judge pointing out that this was really a matter for the contract between the players and the employers. However, players and their agents have paid more and more attention to the protection of their publicity rights.

The last, and perhaps most interesting, potential claimant is the organizer of the competition. In non-team sport such as tennis, the tournament organizer seeks to control the broadcast rights. If the organizer owns a facility (for example, the All England Lawn Tennis and Croquet Association, which runs the Wimbledon championship, owns the courts), then this is little different from the first case. If the organizer pays to hire a facility, then control over broadcast rights will be agreed contractually. In the American major league team sports, the "league organizer" is no more than a joint venture between the owners of the clubs, and therefore has no significance as an independent economic actor (even if the commissioner makes decisions with an economic impact, the commissioner does not share directly in the revenue generated by the league).

However, where a sport is controlled by a governing body that also happens to organize a competition, such as the NCAA's March Madness or the UEFA Champions' League, these governing bodies claim not only to decide about the structure of competition, they also claim a share of the revenue as organizers. Governing bodies are almost never profit-making entities in their own right; rather they organize competitions and take a share of the revenue with the intention of promoting the sport or the participating organizations more widely. Perhaps the best example is the International Olympic Committee (IOC), which awards the games to a city in a member country, negotiates broadcast rights, and retains a substantial share of the revenue to spend on its own activities. The role of governing bodies in sport is highly controversial. In many ways they are a force for good, fostering the development of a sport and redistributing money to less-privileged sections of society. However, the large sums of money at stake have made some of those who run governing bodies unable to resist the temptation to profit personally.

More philosophically, we may ask whether the championship organizer has an ownership right over the broadcast of a game played between two member clubs. On the one hand, the organizer contributes little once the championship is set up, and the clubs do most of the work. On the other, the value of a "friendly" game between two teams is generally much less than a championship game, suggesting that the league organizer adds some value.

In many legal jurisdictions the question of ownership has never been settled. In England a court case was heard in 1999 over the right of clubs in the English Premier League to collectively sell their broadcast rights, and the case was decided without the tribunal ever reaching a decision on who in fact owned the games. Since there was no dispute that the clubs assigned their rights in the games to the league management committee and were paid out of whatever revenue was generated, and because no one doubted that the clubs could do this or suggested that someone else was entitled to a share of the revenue, the court was able to sidestep the question of who owned the rights. In many jurisdictions (such as the United States) it has been decided by the courts that the owner of the stadium owns the rights.

How sports leagues and competition organizers have understood the notion of ownership has affected the way in which leagues have evolved. In baseball the major league teams have jealously guarded their ownership rights over the years, essentially seeing TV as an extension of the home gate. Before the advent of broadcasting, dominant teams tended to hail from large cities, reflecting the economic muscle of larger markets. Baseball's approach simply entrenched that dominance.

In 1950 the average revenue of the sixteen major league baseball teams was $1.6 million, while the Yankees made $2.9 million, 80 percent more than the average. In 2004 the average major league franchise generated revenue of $142 million, while the Yankees made $264 million, 86 percent more than the average. Back in 1950 most generated little more than 10 percent of their revenue from selling (radio) broadcast rights, with upwards of 80 percent of revenue coming from ticket sales. By 2004 gate receipts accounted for only 36 percent of total revenue. For the weakest teams, gate receipts now constitute a small fraction of revenue, with most of the teams in the bottom half of the league generating less than one-third of their revenue from the gate. While the Yankees and the other big teams still make more than 50 percent of their revenue from the gate takings, the smaller teams have tended to see the expansion of local broadcast contracts as the biggest threat to their ability to compete for players. The Yankees own 38 percent of the YES Network, whose primary business is broadcasting Yankee games within and around the New York metropolitan area. YES generates around $200 million per year, and the Yankees' share gives the team a substantial boost to its financial muscle.

These figures illustrate the ways in which broadcasting, especially on television, has enhanced the revenue potential of sports leagues. Even allowing for inflation, baseball's $1.6 million average would be equivalent to only $12.5 million in today's money, less than one-tenth of the revenue generated by the average franchise today (of which there are now thirty). Back in 1950 baseball was already long established as the nation's most popular sport, but television made a baseball game accessible to millions outside the stadium who could be charged indirectly by obliging them to sit through advertising breaks. If the team owners initially feared that broadcasting baseball would undermine interest in attending the game, the effect in the long run turned out to be the reverse. By enabling more and more fans to become involved in watching Major League Baseball, television enhanced the value of tickets to watch the game in person. Both ticket prices and attendance have risen dramatically over the last fifty years. In 1950 the average ticket price was about $1.50, equivalent to about $13.50 in today's money, whereas the average MLB ticket price in 2007 was reported to be $22.69. Over the same period total annual attendance of major league franchises rose from 17 million to nearly 80 million.

Baseball is just one example among many of the transformational power of television. The same can be said of

American football, basketball, soccer, tennis, and golf. However, the way in which television has enriched sports (financially speaking at least) has changed over the years and differs between sports. Technical advances in television have transformed the relationship between the broadcasters and sports. When TV first came on the scene, it was only possible to broadcast three or so channels simultaneously. This meant that TV stations had limited capacity to show events and hence competition for airtime was intense. When competition is mostly on the side of the sellers, prices tend to be low, and so it was with the value of broadcast rights in the early days. Technological innovation, mainly in the form of cable services, has reversed the situation, and households can have access to hundreds of channels. As a result, owners of content, such as attractive sports events, find themselves in demand from competing broadcast services, and the value of rights has exploded. Back in 1950 baseball in total was making only $4 million from the sale of broadcast rights, and even in 1980 the total was only $80 million per season. By 2005 the figure was in the region of $1 billion. This is equivalent to a doubling of broadcast revenue every eight years.

By and large, television has adapted to the needs of baseball. Football, however, adapted to the needs of television. Television changed American society in the 1950s, just as it did European society in the 1960s and most of the rest of the world in the 1970s and 1980s. Nowhere is this truth more evident than in sports. In 1949, 42 million people went to watch minor league baseball; by 1961 the number had fallen to a mere 10 million. By contrast, the average attendance at an NFL game in 1950 was 23,356, but had nearly doubled to 43,617 by 1959. The NFL was on TV; minor league baseball wasn't. Pro football had been established since the 1920s, but never had the cachet of its collegiate cousin. Football had an image as a brutal game, lacking in strategy and amounting to little more than an orchestrated slugfest. Fans of college football often cared more about their alma mater than the action on the field. Television changed that.

In fact, more fundamentally, the technology of recording games changed that. Pro football became a more sophisticated spectacle because of the innovative approach of coaches such as Vince Lombardi, who in the early 1950s would take a Polaroid picture of the opposing team's defensive alignment from the press box and lower it by a pulley down to coaches on the field so that they could adjust the offense. Lombardi was also among the coaches who looked at films of games in order to plan strategy. In other words, pro football took advantage of evolving technology to develop a more sophisticated game, and this is what television viewers started to watch from the 1950s onward. NFL team owners had from the start a more collectivist mind-set in relation to TV. Perhaps this stemmed from the history of the league—over the previous quarter of a century they had already driven off four competing pro leagues that had entered the market—and would drive off a few more in the ensuing years.

In the early years NFL owners agreed that each team should sell the rights to its own games, but they also inserted a clause (Article X) in the league rules that prevented rival teams from broadcasting games into a team's home territory (within seventy-five miles of the stadium), whether or not the team was playing at home that weekend. This rule was in fact simply an extension of the blackout rule, by which each team chose not to sell rights to broadcast its home games when the stadium was not sold out. The Justice Department challenged Article X under the antitrust rules, and in 1953 the Supreme Court affirmed that blackouts could only apply when the home team was in town. The court's ruling restricted the freedom of the teams to enter into further agreements about broadcasting, just when the owners were coming to realize that they had much to gain from presenting a united front. By the mid-1950s all of the individual team contracts were held by CBS and coordinated through commissioner Bert Bell. Bell insisted, on behalf of the owners, that CBS insert a clause in the TV contracts that prohibited showing injuries and fights. Bell was also an apostle of competitive balance, being credited with the creation of the NFL draft and authorship of the famous phrase, "On any given Sunday, any team can beat any other team."

When Bell died in 1959 he was replaced by the young general manager of the L.A. Rams, Pete Rozelle. Rozelle is nowadays given much of the credit for turning the NFL into the world's most successful sports league, and much of that has to do with TV. He inherited a flourishing league, but also inherited a problem, in the form of the newly created American Football League. The AFL was sponsored by a disgruntled Lamar Hunt, who had been unable to buy an NFL franchise despite several attempts. As a smart sports entrepreneur, Hunt recognized the value of TV. Unlike most expansion leagues in the past, which had concentrated on breaking into the big cities, the AFL was mostly built around medium-sized cities. Instead of relying primarily on gate revenue, the AFL signed a collective deal with ABC to show a "game of the week." The AFL also agreed to share the broadcast revenue equally between the teams, creating a significant cushion against falling attendance.

This provoked the NFL to sign their own collective contract, only to discover that the court's decision back in 1953 prevented them from doing so. Thus the league went to Congress and persuaded the politicians to pass the Sports Broadcasting Act in 1961, exempting collective selling of broadcast rights to free-to-air TV networks from antitrust scrutiny. With the legal obstacle out of the way, Rozelle started to re-create the American TV landscape, with the NFL as its centerpiece. Football had already transformed Sunday afternoon programming, traditionally a desert for the TV companies. Then the 1966 merger agreement between the NFL and AFL led to the inaugural Super Bowl in 1967, and ultimately Monday Night Football in 1970. The genius of the NFL was to recognize that TV wanted more than a game, it wanted a myth and a spectacle of Hollywood proportions, an "appointment to view" and an epic narrative. Since the 1960s the NFL has led the sports world by presenting a unified "brand image" while investing in the most innovative film technologies. Its reward has been to become the most valuable sports league in the world. Since 2006 the annual broadcast revenue of the NFL has been around $3.7 billion (about three times as much as MLB).

The relationship between sport and television now seems so central to any account of modern society that it is hard to remember that this development seemed far from inevitable in the early days. Originally most established sports were wary of TV, fearing that it would undermine attendance at games. This fear still haunts even the mighty NFL, which continues to adhere to the blackout rule. Major sports were often slow to recognize that they can benefit from the extended publicity that national TV coverage brings, while broadcasters have often been wary of the smaller sports. In the early days there was a certain snobbishness among TV executives about sports coverage, and much concern about the educational mission of the medium. Picture quality also led many to be skeptical about the possibilities of following baseballs and footballs on the small screen. These skeptics have largely been proved wrong by executives who recognized both the entertainment value of contests and the marketing potential of sports stars.

Marxist critics have argued that modern sports are simply the new "opium of the people," diverting attention from the problems in people's own lives while offering capitalists ways to sell more products and extract more profit. There seems to be a grain of truth in this. The extraordinary reach of sports into the lives of most people, and the willingness of so many people to identify with sports stars and translate that identification into the purchase of a pair of shoes or some other piece of branded merchandise suggests a powerful link between sporting culture and product markets. The Marxists seem mistaken, however, when they imagine that this marketing is a premeditated conspiracy on the part of the capitalists. Were this true, we would be able to trace the evolution of the sports business through the conscious plans of media executives and sports league organizers to lead viewers into the consumption of branded goods associated with sports. In truth, the whole process has been random, and somewhat surprising even to those closely involved with it.

Nowhere is this point more clearly emphasized than in the case of ESPN, the iconic symbol of the penetration of sports into our daily lives. ESPN was launched as a twenty-four-hour sport broadcasting network in 1979. It was the brainchild of Bill Rasmussen, a visionary sports nut with no track record in broadcasting. Pretty much every major network executive laughed in his face when he tried to tout his idea around the media industry. In the end he secured funding from Getty Oil, a company with no prior experience of broadcasting. ESPN started broadcasting on a shoestring, with virtually no sports programming and certainly unable to fill twenty-four hours a day. It grew largely thanks to the willingness of its sports-mad employees to make do and deal with conditions that regular TV people would never tolerate; and even then, ESPN was nearly bankrupted on more than one occasion. The secret of ESPN's success resided in a single lucky break. Right at the beginning Rasmussen was able to sign a deal to rent a satellite transponder, which could be used to broadcast to local cable stations. At the time, the networks had not realized the value of the satellite capacity, and had not bought it up. The industry realized its mistake literally days after the lease to ESPN, and but for those few days, ESPN would not even have been technically feasible. For an initial $10 million investment in 1979, Getty was able to sell the network in 1984 for $230 million. By 1995, when 80 percent of the business was acquired by Disney, ESPN was valued at $5 billion; according to a report by UBS in 2007, ESPN's value had escalated to $28 billion, about 40 percent of Disney's net worth.

Clearly, those who controlled TV in the 1960s and 1970s significantly underestimated the appetite of American TV audiences for sport. Until then government regulation had effectively protected the free-to-air national networks from the competitive threat offered by local cable services. The networks focused on premium sports that would attract large audiences, which in turn would attract the advertisers. The deregulation of the cable industry at the end of the 1970s led to an explosion of local sports programming, including college sports and then high school sports. Cable's appetite for programming has significantly enlarged the universe of sports that people watch, and has brought formerly obscure sports such as NASCAR to national prominence. At the same time coverage of traditionally popular events has deepened, with longer prematch buildups, postmatch debriefings, and in-depth coverage of seemingly nontelevisual events such as the NFL draft. Between 1980 and 2000 the networks doubled the number of program hours devoted to sports to around two thousand hours. This, however, is dwarfed by cable coverage, which went from essentially nothing to seventeen thousand hours over the same period. In many cases the owners of the content were only too happy to showcase their sport to local and national audiences.

Others resisted, sometimes illegally. As was mentioned in chapter 3, for many years the NCAA restricted the broadcasting of college football to no more than a handful of the big games for fear that broadcasting would destroy attendance at the lesser college games. This restriction was successfully challenged under the antitrust laws by Oklahoma University in 1984, leading to the dramatic expansion of broadcasting of college sports. Moreover, the fears of the NCAA do not seem to have been realized, with attendance increasing over the last two decades rather than falling. This seems to be a pattern that repeats itself every time sports broadcasting comes before the courts. Restrictions are challenged on the grounds that consumers are being denied access to attractive programming (either by the owners of the content who are being restrained or by the antitrust authority); the restriction is defended by a sports organization on the grounds that increased exposure on TV could damage the sport; the sports organization loses the case, which results in increased exposure that then leads in turn to increased demand.

Outside of the United States the evolution of sports and TV has been complicated by the deeper involvement of the state in the management of broadcasting. The United States was almost alone in licensing radio and television broadcasting to private enterprises; everywhere else in the world the government deemed control of the new medium too sensitive to be left in private hands, and therefore state broadcasting corporations were established. For example, in the UK the publicly funded BBC was created in 1926 to deliver radio broadcasts according to a charter laid down by Parliament. This monopoly was justified in part on the grounds that there was a need to maintain a uniform programming policy that would fulfill the charter objective to "inform, educate and entertain." From its inception the BBC claimed (as it still does today) to observe a policy of strict impartiality, although this begs the question of who decides what is impartial (in 1938 the BBC rejected requests by Winston Churchill to broadcast a speech denouncing the government policy of appeasing the Nazis, on the grounds that his views were too extreme). It was not until 1955 that the UK government licensed a commercial TV station, and commercial radio stations were not permitted until 1973.

The BBC was decidedly highbrow, and from the beginning demonstrated little interest in sports programming. It did make the first UK radio broadcasts of soccer and cricket matches in 1927 (regular broadcasting of cricket had started in Australia in 1924), but soon discovered that soccer clubs, fearing the loss of gate receipts, wanted payment to allow their games to be broadcast. Unwilling to spend public money in this way, BBC radio and later TV restricted itself mainly to highlights of soccer, giving fuller coverage to the more gentlemanly and more inexpensive cricket. Even the advent of commercial TV in the UK did not produce a big enough offer to put live league soccer on TV. However, from the 1950s the development of the World Cup, and the desire to follow the fortunes of the national team, generated at least some live soccer on TV. At a time when the U.S. networks were paying hundreds of millions of dollars to show live baseball and football, there was no live coverage in England of the Football League.

As in the United States, a revolution took place in the 1980s. On the one hand the soccer clubs finally reconciled themselves to the loss of gate and agreed in 1982 to sell their games for live coverage. Initially this was limited to a handful of games, and the payments were tiny—amounting to no more than a few thousand pounds per club in the early years. However, this all changed dramatically with the advent of satellite broadcasting in the mid-1980s. Satellite broadcasting created competition for the existing terrestrial broadcasting cartels, and sports rights soon became the battleground. Competition for Football League rights in 1988 caused their value to increase fourfold over the previous contract, but it was in 1992 that the real revolution took place, with the creation of the FA Premier League and the sales of its rights to Rupert Murdoch's Sky satellite broadcasting corporation. To some people the advent of satellite broadcasting represented a step backward; after all, prior to 1992 live league soccer could be watched on free-to-air TV, while since 1992 consumers have had to pay a subscription to watch. However,

Sky paid much larger fees, which rose from £49 million (about $90 million) per season between 1992 and 1996 to £550 million (about $1 billion) per season in 2006. A subscription to Sky Sports is expensive—costing up to £50 per month ($90) depending on the exact range of services purchased. This revenue has done much to increase the wages of players, but it has also helped to provide security for investment in upgrading stadiums, which has been substantial in the past fifteen years. Moreover, the number of live games that fans can see on TV increased from around 18 games before 1992 to 138 by 2000 (although still well below the total of 380 played in a season).

There seems to be a significant difference in the cost of live sports programming in the UK and the United States. Moreover, the evolution I have described was replicated across most of Europe. Free-to-air broadcasters, whether state owned or commercially licensed, proved unable to compete with premium pay TV services in Europe, whereas in the United States most of the premium rights (for example, Super Bowl, World Series) have either remained on free-to-air services or are available on basic cable services for a minimal fee. European governments became so concerned about the political implications of the migration of popular sports programming to pay TV that they passed antisiphoning laws to restrict certain premium events to free-to-air (for example, Wimbledon, the Tour de France, the World Cup, and the Olympic Games).

Since all of these sports rights are sold through auction, what requires explanation is the inability of terrestrial broadcasters to win auctions in Europe when their American counterparts are able to do so. There seem to be two main factors contributing to this asymmetry. First, sports programming in the United States is more valuable to a free-to-air broadcaster since regulators permit a larger number of advertising minutes per hour (in the United States fifteen are permitted, whereas in the European Union the number is generally around eight). This is a consequence of regulation, but it is also the case that American sports have been more willing to create advertising breaks in sports (for example, the two-minute warning in football) where the rule-making bodies of sports such as soccer have been unwilling to change. The second factor at work is the Sports Broadcasting Act. In the United States collective selling is permitted only if the rights are sold free-to-air; in Europe collective selling is permitted in some countries (UK, France, Germany) and not permitted in others (Italy, Spain) but the treatment of free-to-air and pay TV is always the same. Leagues can typically generate more revenue through collective selling, and this has given free-to-air networks in the United States a government-supported competitive advantage.

Collective selling became an issue in the United States in the 1950s as the value of sports broadcast rights started to escalate. When the value of rights exploded in Europe in the 1990s, the same legal issues went to court. In Europe the league typically represented not just the member clubs, but the entire sport from school and amateur level right up to the highest professional level. In France federations are delegated by the state to organize leagues and championships in each sport and therefore enjoy the privileges of a state monopoly. In most other European countries federations are independent bodies that claim the promotion of their sport as their primary activity. On these grounds they have often demanded exemption from competition law, but the European Court of Justice ruled many years ago that insofar as sports organizations engage in commercial activities, they must be governed by the same laws of competition as any ordinary business. Without an equivalent of the Sports Broadcasting Act, competition authorities in England, Germany, Italy, Spain, and the Netherlands all examined the sale of league soccer rights during the 1990s. Furthermore, the European Commission, acting on behalf of the member states, also undertook an examination of the sale of broadcast rights to Formula One motor racing and the UEFA Champions League.

In general the courts have been preoccupied with two issues. The first is whether collective selling represents an exploitation of monopoly power by a cartel, or whether the special status of a league, either as single entity or joint venture, means that collective selling merely enables the league to sell a better product. The second issue is whether the sale of rights collectively restricts the development of competition in broadcast markets. In general the second issue tended to outweigh the first. The problem was that broadcasters such as Sky in Britain, Kirch in Germany, and Canal+ in France soon recognized that premium sports content (such as soccer and Formula One in Europe) was the key to establishing a strong broadcasting service, and so set about acquiring valuable collections of rights. Rupert Murdoch famously described sports rights such as soccer as the "battering ram" that would open the market to new services. However, what the European Union wanted was competition in pay TV, not a set of new monopolies, particularly when the free-to-air competitors turned out to be so weak. On this view, if clubs were obliged to sell rights individually, then all the competing pay-TV broadcasters would be able to get a share.

The leagues defended themselves by arguing that collective sale was necessary to showcase the league as a whole (much the same rationale advanced by the NFL nearly fifty years earlier), and further adding that the money it generated would be used to support the weaker clubs and invest in the "grass roots." This cross-subsidy argument has always been extremely popular with politicians, who see an alternative source of funding for organizations that frequently demand public funds. This is in general a very dangerous argument. If it were valid, then it would be possible to justify any monopoly abuse by donating some of the proceeds to charity. Despite this, the argument tends to carry some weight with judges. Overall, the outcome on collective selling across Europe has been mixed. In Germany the court decided against collective selling, at which point the league obtained an antitrust exemption from the German parliament. In Spain and Italy the government mandated individual selling, largely at the behest of dominant clubs such as Juventus, AC Milan, Barcelona, and Real Madrid. In England collective selling was upheld by the court, and despite further investigations by the European Commission, it remains in place today. Finally, at the level of the European Union, collective deals were accepted for Formula One and the UEFA Champions League, subject to a number of safeguards.

As in the United States, broadcasting of sport in Europe has produced pressures to restructure competition in order to meet the demands of broadcasters, but the reaction in Europe has been quite different. The professional major league sports in the United States are run by men (and a few, but not many, women) who would be proud to call themselves *business*men. Their reaction to the advent of TV was the same as any businessperson to a new technology: how will it help the development of my *business?* While different sports may have thought that different business models were appropriate to the exploitation of television's potential, all of them were primarily interested in the extra *profits* that TV would generate for them. In Europe people who run clubs and leagues tend not to think of themselves as businessmen first and foremost, even if they have come to accept that the business side of the sport can help them. In this respect sports organizers in Europe might be considered more like university chancellors of successful NCAA teams. However, instead of feeling their obligation first and foremost to an academic institution, team directors and owners in Europe feel their allegiance lies with the club, the location, and the community in which it resides (this is one reason why team relocation has never been an issue in Europe). This does not mean that sport and business need conflict. Extra revenue from broadcasting can help a team and benefit a university or a community.

However, sometimes conflicts do emerge. In the United States the professional sports have evolved in response to changes in the demographics of the country. While these sports started in the northeast of the country, expansion has moved the leagues south and west to meet the demands of the most rapidly growing parts of the country. At the same time, the leagues have evolved competitive structures to ensure that the best players can meet in competition. In Europe, leagues have developed along national lines, with each country having its own top league. From the 1950s international club competitions developed as an adjunct to the normal domestic calendar of games. Since these games allowed the best players from different countries to meet, these competitions became extremely popular, the most successful today being the European Champions League. Since the 1980s many of the larger clubs have argued that commercial logic and the demands of TV suggest expansion of European-wide competition and a reduction in the significance of national championships (in much the same way that in the United States minor league baseball effectively collapsed in the 1950s and was supplanted by TV sports such as the NFL).

The bigger clubs have gone a long way toward creating a structure that enables the top European teams to meet in competition on a regular basis, but they are still a long way behind the United States. For example, over recent years the two biggest clubs in Spain have been Real Madrid and Barcelona; in Italy it has been Juventus and AC Milan; in Germany, Bayern Munich and Borussia Dortmund; and in England, Manchester United and Chelsea (with apologies to fans of other clubs). Each pair meets at least twice a year in domestic competition, and sometimes meets in the Champions League. But how often do they meet foreign rivals? If they each played each other once a season, this would generate twenty-four games, or 120 times over five seasons. But in fact over the years 2002 to 2006 these teams only met each other a total of twenty-six times. They employ the top stars, and usually when they do play, they draw sellout crowds and enormous TV audiences. While the clubs themselves would like to play each other more often, the national associations veto this possibility. The clubs could (and sometimes do) threaten to form a new league among themselves, but one factor that holds them back is a loyalty to the traditions of the sport. More recently, leagues have started to think about merging across national boundaries; for example, many of the top clubs in Belgium and the Netherlands would like to unite in a single league but are prevented from doing so by the rigid national demarcation of sports in Europe. Again, the clubs could leave the "football family," but choose not to do so.

Nonetheless, the potential size of the TV audiences for these enhanced products is creating more and more pressure to bring about the necessary changes. One possibility is that Rupert Murdoch might do again what he did in Australia in 1995. Back then he wanted to obtain broadcast rights to the rugby league, one of the most popular sports in Australia. Failing to win the rights at auction, he set up his own Super League in parallel with the existing league and spent a fortune hiring the best players. After two seasons of financial meltdown, the rival league sued for peace and Murdoch got his broadcast rights. Illustrating Murdoch's commitment to winning, this story also shows how the value of viewing audiences transforms sport; what mattered in this case was not what the fans or the administrators wanted, but where the largest audiences lay and who had the financial muscle to seize the market. In the United States the inevitable victory of "market forces" has long been accepted in sports as it has elsewhere; in Europe it remains to be seen whether politicians will seek to swim against the tide.

The problems faced by administrators, who consider themselves entrusted with the well-being of sport, that arise from the commercial pressures associated with TV are amply demonstrated by the world's two biggest sports TV events: the FIFA World Cup and the Olympic Games. The organizers claim to reach TV audiences that run into the billions, although in reality this only refers to the number of people who potentially could watch the event on a TV, not those actually watching. Yet audiences for these events are huge, and the broadcasting rights, together with the associated sponsorship rights, are the principal sources of revenue for the bodies that govern these activities (FIFA and the International Olympic Committee). On the one hand, these bodies have used part of the revenue to fund the development of sport internationally. FIFA has had notable successes in funding the development of soccer in Asia and especially in Africa. The IOC has undertaken a wide range of developmental work and done much to bring the practice of sport to poorer communities. On the other hand, these bodies have been dogged by tales of corruption, many of which have been substantiated.

These bodies also face increasing pressure to distribute more of the revenue to those who provide the entertainment. Olympic athletes have not yet demanded payment for participation in the Games, but FIFA has long allocated money to national associations, which in turn have paid players for playing in the World Cup. While this has led to some disputes (in 2006 the Togo players threatened not to play a game in the World Cup because they did not trust the Togo FA to pay them; in the end FIFA agreed to guarantee the payment so the match could be played), the main issue today is compensation for the clubs. The clubs that employ the players are obliged under the rules of their national association to release them without compensation to play in games representing their country, many of which generate substantial sums from gate receipts and TV rights. In 2006 the clubs launched a challenge in the European Court of Justice, demanding compensation for player release. Eventually the case was settled out of court,

with the clubs claiming to have gained significant concessions from the governing bodies.

If broadcasting has transformed sport, it is not done
yet. In the coming decades the development of TV sports
in Asia will become increasingly significant. Until the
1990s serious interest in TV sport was limited mainly to
Japan. Since then, however, interest in soccer has grown
in countries such as Malaysia, Thailand, and above all
China. Currently this interest has manifested itself most
significantly in a series of match-fixing scandals associated with gambling syndicates in China. Formula One
has for many years run Grand Prix in Asia to meet the interest of that market, and tennis and golf tournaments in
Asia have attracted big stars and large audiences. The Yao
Ming phenomenon has also created significant interest in
the NBA in China. As television spreads, and purchasing
power of Asians increases, their demand for sports will
play a bigger and bigger role in dictating which sports are
represented on TV. In 2008 the Beijing Olympics demonstrated the immense enthusiasm for sport in China, fueled by the home nation's success in topping the gold
medal count. In the same year the creation of a new cricket
competition in India, the Indian Premier League, which
was able to attract most of the world's top players on the
back of a $1 billion broadcasting contract with Sony,
demonstrated the capacity of emerging markets with large
television populations to take a growing share of the global
sports market.

Technology also has a big part to play in the future.
Selling sports content on the Internet and on mobile
phones represents new commercial opportunities, and
some sports are already beginning to exploit them. It remains to be seen how these will affect consumers in the

long run. Until now the goal of sports programmers has been to find events that will stand out in the calendar so the audiences will make space in their schedules to sit down and watch. As the volume of content has increased, a large amount of it has come to be seen as "disposable"— available if there is nothing better to do—while only a small number of events have retained real cachet. With the Internet and mobile phones, sport might move to a world where it is "always on," like popular music, there in the background at work or on the move. Interactive gaming is bringing a new dimension to rotisserie leagues and fantasy sports. Of course, how this ultimately works out will depend on where the most money is to be made.

Six

SPORTS AND THE PUBLIC PURSE

On June 19, 1999, the citizens of Sion, Switzerland, assembled in the town square for a party. Together they watched on a huge TV screen the proceedings of the 109th plenary session of the International Olympic Committee in Seoul, South Korea. At stake was the awarding of the 2006 Winter Games. Six months previously the bids of each of the competing cities had been evaluated by an IOC technical committee, and the evaluation report had identified Sion as the most suitable site. Following the scandal surrounding the awarding of the 2002 winter games to Salt Lake City, Olympic delegates were no longer allowed to visit the host cities. Instead, each city had to make a presentation at the plenary, but neither the bookmakers nor the good people of Sion had any doubts.

Later that evening the Swiss remembered who had admitted there was corruption in the Salt Lake City bidding process—none other than Switzerland's most prominent member of the IOC, Marc Hodler. The 2006 games had been awarded to Turin, Italy. Revenge? No one in Sion had any doubts.

The catalog of corrupt activities that were uncovered in the Salt Lake City scandal is extraordinary. Like Sion, Salt Lake City had bid before and lost. Eager to learn from their mistakes, its representatives realized, like many others before them, that the quality of their proposal mattered less than bribes to the IOC. The nature of these bribes was well known to officials and journalists connected to the Olympic circus. Shopping trips for wives, expensive vacations, and reimbursement of first-class airfares (sometimes more than once) were simply the most basic. More remarkable were paying fees for the children of delegates at expensive U.S. academies and the extortion of personal "loans." Most creative, perhaps, was the ploy of the delegate who would arrive at a host city and report to the police that $20,000 in cash had been stolen from his room, refusing all offers to pursue investigations; either the city took the hint and paid up $20,000 or his support was lost. Apparently he tried the scam in several cities around the world. The trouble was, many of the potential hosts were willing to pay, so prestigious is the hosting of the Olympic Games.

About the same time that the Salt Lake City boosters were handing out bribes to IOC members, senior executives in a number of American companies were engaged in a different kind of fraud. Subsequent investigations showed that from at least 1999 onward executives at companies such as Enron, Tyco, and MCI WorldCom were misrepresenting the financial position of the businesses they managed. By doing so they were able to write contracts, take over rival businesses, and generate millions of dollars in salaries for themselves. In order to perpetrate this fraud they usually needed their accountants to support their deception, either tacitly or explicitly, the payoff for the accountants being fat audit fees and lucrative consultancy contracts. Within a few years these frauds were exposed by the financial failure of the businesses in question. Jobs were lost, pension funds of honest employees vanished, and Congress quickly set about doing something to meet the public disquiet. The result was the Sarbanes-Oxley

Act in 2002. The act established the Public Company Accounting Oversight Board, to ensure that accounting rules were properly observed; made senior executives personally liable for any misrepresentation of the company's financial position in the accounts; and mandated lengthier prison sentences for executives found guilty of misrepresentation. Many other countries have followed the American lead in tightening up the control of corporations and the activities of the managers who run them.

Not surprisingly, those executives who oversaw the corrupt activities at companies such as MCI and Enron were removed from their positions and in many cases tried for fraud. Because senior managers at Arthur Andersen, then one of the big five global accounting firms, were implicated in the frauds, the company surrendered its licenses to operate and had to be liquidated. Bernie Ebbers, the CEO of WorldCom, was found guilty of fraud and sentenced to twenty-five years in prison. Kenneth Lay, the CEO of Enron, was also found guilty on six counts of fraud and died of a heart attack before he could be sentenced.

Dave Johnson and Tom Welch, the leaders of the Salt Lake City Olympic bid committee, were also indicted by the Justice Department, on fifteen counts of fraud. (They were acquitted on all counts.) But what of the IOC itself? Its members had accepted bribes, and statements by senior members such as Marc Hodler suggested that they knew such activities took place, but had never obtained proof. Following an internal inquiry, six members identified with some of the most egregious payoffs were expelled, leaving more than one hundred other members untouched. None of those expelled faced any further sanctions, and presumably kept all of the bribes they had received over the years. Not one member of the IOC's executive board was dismissed, nor was any action taken against the president, Juan Antonio Samaranch, who retired in 2001 after being created life president. All in all, those involved in Olympic fraud got off much more lightly than those guilty of corporate fraud.

How are we to explain this? Some lawyers might say that it is a matter of jurisdiction. American companies are subject to American law, and Congress was sufficiently concerned about the scandals to change the law and impose big penalties on corrupt businessmen. By contrast, the IOC is an association domiciled in Switzerland and regulated by the Swiss law of association, which is, to say the least, permissive. Essentially, Swiss law permits the IOC to make up its own rules and to govern itself, with no interference from the state (just for good measure, it is exempt from taxation). The United States Olympic Committee (USOC) was created by Congress to oversee the organization of the U.S. Olympic teams, and was given the right to control the use of the five-ring Olympic symbol in the United States, but the USOC was not directly involved in the Salt Lake scandal. The bribes were handed out by the Salt Lake City Organizing Committee and taken by IOC members.

However, this legal account does not really get to the bottom of the different penalties imposed in the two scandals. The U.S. Congress is quite happy to pass laws that imply jurisdiction over the actions of foreigners living outside the United States, and indeed several foreigners have been extradited to stand trial in the United States in relation to the collapse of Enron. But when John McCain demanded that Samaranch appear before his Commerce Committee in 1999 to talk about corruption in the IOC, he declined to attend. Could Congress take on the Olympic movement? Maybe, but there would be a high price to pay. The Summer Olympics continue to be one of the biggest draws on TV. For Athens 2004, NBC, which paid $793 million to buy the broadcast rights and claimed to air twelve hundred hours of coverage, achieved ratings of around 15 percent of the U.S. TV viewing audience— better than most of the top ten entertainment shows on the networks. Although Beijing 2008 got even higher ratings, when the Olympics are held in the United States, the ratings soar to 25 percent. The winter Olympic figure skating finals in 1994 (the famous competition between Nancy Kerrigan and Tonya Harding) ranks sixth in all-time U.S. TV ratings . Any institution enjoying this level of popularity will always be treated with respect by elected politicians.

Today, one of the most interesting competitions in the world of sport is the competition to host the Olympic Games. The games are awarded to a city, but it has long been necessary to have the backing of the national government to win. The IOC formalized this position in the bidding for the 2012 summer games by requiring a government guarantee underwriting the costs of hosting the games. Governments, or rather the politicians who make the decisions, are more than willing to do this since bringing the games to your country carries enormous prestige. Only the FIFA World Cup generates as much international attention as the Olympic Games.

Of course, the Olympics also generate a huge amount of money, from the sale of television rights, the sale of sponsorship rights, merchandising, and ticketing. Over the last four-year Olympic cycle (2001–2004) the IOC generated over $4 billion; more than half of this came from the global sale of broadcast rights and one-third from sponsorship. Given all of this revenue, one might wonder why the games need to be underwritten by government. This is not merely a matter of a contingency: the problem is that as a free-standing venture, the Olympic Games run at a loss. Now, this is an astonishing fact. How can you lose money on an event that lasts for three weeks, rewards its performers with nothing more than a medal tied with a bit of ribbon, and generates billions of dollars of revenue? There is really only one answer: the Olympics are staged far more lavishly than necessary because the IOC can induce host cities and governments to underwrite most of the costs while keeping for itself a large part of the revenues.

Olympic accounting is a dark art, and tracing all the flows of money is never easy. In many cases government keeps the precise figures well hidden from public view (for example, China gave little public information about the costs of Beijing 2008). But roughly speaking it goes like this. According to the Greek government, staging the 2004 Olympics in Athens cost about $11.5 billion. However, the Athens 2004 Organizing Committee (ATHOC) generated only a little over $2 billion in revenue from the games. Mostly this was revenue from TV and sponsorship, with the rest coming from tickets and related sources. Crucially, Athens received only about 50 percent of the TV and sponsorship money, the rest being retained by the IOC for distribution to Olympic committees in other countries, to develop sport and cover the IOC's own considerable administrative expenses. So the Greek government was left to pick up the tab amounting to a cool $9 to $10 billion. Even though this was offset by some subsidies from the European Union, it still made a big dent in the

Greek economy, whose total annual revenue is only $200 billion. In other words, Greece hosted a party that cost 5 percent of its annual revenue, or just over $2000 for every person in the working population!

The spending on the games can be divided into two parts—operating expenses related to the day-to-day management of the event, and capital expenses relating to the construction of Olympic facilities. The ATHOC budget covered the operating costs with a little bit to spare, allowing some of the more optimistic commentators to observe that the games had actually made a profit. This would make sense if the Olympic infrastructure could be sold off at cost to investors, but the truth is somewhat more depressing. We should separate the capital budget into three further parts: infrastructure relating directly to staging Olympic events (stadiums, costing around $3 billion), the Olympic village ($1.5 billion), and public infrastructure relating to the city and its surroundings, such as roads, railways, and airports (about $5 billion).

The Greeks built thirty-six new facilities to host the games, from the huge Olympic stadium and the Olympic Aquatic Center down to the more modest Vouliagmeni Olympic Center, holding twenty-two hundred spectators for the men's and women's triathlon. No plans were made for these facilities after the Olympics, and most of them were locked up after the games ended. It was not until 2005 that a plan was published for use of the centers, and the government decided to declare, naturally enough, that they would primarily be used for sports. Two years after the games, most of the sites had not been sold off and were still on offer at public auction; the problem is that there is not much demand in Athens for specialized sporting facilities. Meanwhile, maintenance costs $100 million a year. In 2008 one report claimed that twenty-one out of twenty-two facilities investigated were derelict. Far from producing a legacy for Athens, the facilities are a burden. If previous Olympics are anything to go by, most of these facilities will be torn down in the end.

The Olympic Village, which housed the athletes during the games, can be converted into around twenty-five hundred houses, giving an average cost of $600,000 per house. It is possible that the government could realize this price, though if the properties were sold, they would be unlikely to generate a substantial profit. Moreover, the World Wildlife Fund pointed out that the village was built on the site of one of the last remaining forests in that part of Greece, an embarrassing environmental debacle.

The road, rail, and airport infrastructure has in general been viewed more positively by most commentators. Athens was famous for the poor quality of its transportation, and the metro system now stretches an impressive distance, the international airport is an attractive modern facility with plenty of capacity, and the road from the airport to the city center is comfortable and efficient. Since there was a need to build this infrastructure in any case, one might argue that the cost should not even be attributed to the Olympics, since it would have been incurred even if the Olympics had not taken place. However, this does not allow for the fact that the total costs escalated from the initial estimate of around $5 billion because of delays and the absolute requirement to complete the project on time. It was a source of much embarrassment to the Greeks that so much had been left to the last minute, and an opportunity for firms and workers to extract huge bonuses to make a superhuman effort to complete the project on time. This effort also cost fourteen lives, as construction rules were ignored in the bid to get things done.

But even if the costs of hosting the games were substantial, many people, probably including a majority of Greeks, will say that the money was well spent. It was of great symbolic importance to bring the games back to their original home, and there is no doubt that the eventual completion of a successful games created a significant "feel-good factor" among the Greeks. But would the Greeks have voted to host the games had it been announced that they would be funded out of a $2,000 tax on every working citizen (GDP per capita is around $19,000)? Perhaps, but national referendums about whether to host the Olympics are unknown. In fact, the politicians involved with trying to attract events such as the Olympic Games claim that they will create a large positive boost to the economy. In this way, large public subsidies can be justified on the grounds that they will produce jobs, growth, and greater long-term prosperity. Before the games some forecasters estimated that the economic boost to the Greek economy would be in the region of $12 to $13 billion, easily outweighing the costs.

Where does this boost come from? The theory can be traced back to John Maynard Keynes, whose analysis of the Depression of the 1930s influenced a generation of policymakers and created the postwar consensus on economic policy. Keynes's theory is a theory of underemployment. During an economic depression, he argued, investors lost confidence in the potential to make profits in the future out of investment today. Such crises of confidence tend to be self-fulfilling, since reluctance to invest translates into increased savings, reduced expenditure, and therefore a depressed economy. In the face of this crisis of confidence, Keynes argued, the only solution is for the government to boost confidence by investing itself. Government spending would put money in the pockets of ordinary people (in the form of wages), which would then get spent on goods and services, stimulating the economy. Moreover, Keynes argued that there would be a ripple effect, since every dollar spent represents a dollar of income for someone else, and that someone will inevitably spend a significant fraction of this income on goods and services. As the dollar circulates in a sequence of transactions from buyers to sellers, it generates more and more economic activity. Keynes dubbed this the "multiplier effect"; depending on how much of every dollar is spent (rather than saved), the multiplier might range from a small number to a very large one indeed. So powerful did Keynes believe this effect to be that he argued that the government did not even need to spend the money on productive jobs—paying people to dig holes and fill them up again would stimulate the economy into growth.

Olympic stadiums that will never be used again are a bit like holes in the ground, and the economic argument for hosting the games relies on these multiplier effects. The Keynesian story dominated global economic policy between 1945 and 1970, but by the end of the 1960s it was running into problems. Economic theorists started to worry more and more about the assumptions underlying the story. First, they wondered why the economy wouldn't right itself without government intervention. After all, if demand for workers fell, so would wages. Cheap wages would make employing workers look more profitable, and this would be a natural route out of recession. Keynes told a story of a "liquidity trap" that would prevent the economy from entering this virtuous circle, but the consensus among economists was that Keynes had got this wrong. More importantly, perhaps, it became clear that large government deficits created by public spending to avoid recession led to higher and higher inflation levels. Milton Friedman pointed out that the policy amounted to little more than printing money, which inevitably leads to higher prices. This in itself seemed to be causing uncertainty and a reluctance to invest, and soon inflation was viewed as a bigger threat than too little spending. Friedman and his followers advocated tight monetary policy to control inflation and free markets to create opportunities for growth, and the relative long-term success of these policies in the 1970s and 1980s caused the simplistic Keynesian ideas to be discarded.

Discarded, I should say, except when it came to investments such as the Olympic Games. Here the "boosters" continued to argue that local economic growth could be stimulated by public spending on infrastructure such as sports stadiums. Athens was typical in this respect. Advocates argued that the construction phase of the games would boost the economy through extra jobs in that industry, while the games themselves would produce additional tourism. Neither of these arguments makes much economic sense.

As we have already seen, Olympic construction is extremely expensive relative to any benefit it produces. The same amount of public (or private) expenditure on ordinary housing or infrastructure, with a guaranteed long-term value, is far more likely to boost the local economy. For example, rather than produce 2,500 luxury houses, the same amount of expenditure could probably have created 5,000 equivalent units without the pressures associated with meeting Olympic specifications and deadlines.

Similarly, an extra $3 billion spent on roads rather than stadiums would probably have done more to stimulate the Athenian economy. This illustrates the principal problem with Keynesian theory—it does not take account of the opportunity cost, meaning how the money could have been spent in the next best alternative. Keynes simply assumed that there was none, because in the absence of government spending, nothing would happen. This may have been true in the 1930s, but it certainly was not true in the Greek economy at the beginning of the new millennium.

To put it another way, the government can always create jobs by spending money, but what is the cost of creating each job? Each type of investment has a different cost, and creating jobs by building state-of-the-art stadiums is one of the most expensive. Economists might also argue that the cheapest jobs to create are those that come from meeting needs expressed by consumers in the market. Whether or not laissez-faire always works better than public spending is still a matter of controversy, but the point does illustrate that there are alternatives. When the government spends money, it tends to displace some of these alternatives. For example, Greek construction workers were moved away from private infrastructure projects into the Olympics. To identify the true impact of Olympic spending, we need to offset the gains to the economy from what was built with what could have been built instead, such as schools, hospitals, and other productive infrastructure. Of course, such calculations are highly speculative, and so the politicians can get away with claiming that there were no better alternatives. In the end, however, it turned out that the Olympics created more jobs than there were employable citizens in Greece; hence a lot of workers had to be imported. These people returned home once the construction was completed, and took their wages with them. So in a sense the Greeks spent money to boost economies other than their own.

The idea that hosting the Olympic Games might attract a lot of visitors who would spend money locally and boost the economy seems much more promising. But the reality is depressing. First, only visitors from outside the country bring an additional benefit to the economy. The Greeks who attended the Olympics brought no extra benefit to the Greek economy because in the absence of the Olympics they would have spent money on other entertainments in Greece, for example by going to the movies. These alternatives lost business because of the Olympics. To boost the economy, the event has to generate spending that is not displaced from elsewhere in the economy; robbing Peter to pay Paul does not make the economy grow. Sadly, it was principally Greeks who went to the games. Negative publicity about delays in construction and fears of terrorism deterred many international visitors who might have attended, and in the end only two-thirds of the 5.3 million tickets available were sold. Broadcasters complained during the games that empty stands were detracting from the spectacle and tried (unsuccessfully) to persuade the organizers to give away unsold tickets. Even worse, the games dented tourist arrivals in Greece in 2004. Over the previous three years visitors to Greece had numbered around 14.8 million. But in 2004 only 13 million people visited—a decline of 12 percent. In 2005 visits increased to 14 million, still well below the pre-Olympics figures. In other words, the Olympic Games *hurt* international tourism in Greece.

Athens is perhaps unusual because of the negative publicity before the games, but there is little evidence that the

Olympics boost tourism in general. One reason is that even foreign tourists are not all additional tourists—many are people who were planning to visit anyway. A second reason is that the scale of the publicity that surrounds these events deters many people. For example, most would-be visitors to Athens want to see the historical sites, and a proportion of these types skipped Athens in 2004 because of the Olympics crowd, perhaps preferring to visit Rome instead. If anything, the evidence suggests that there is a post-games tourist slump, not a boom. After the Sydney games in 2000, numbers of visitors to Australia went into a four-year decline. While supporters of the Sydney games tried to blame other factors, such as new fears of terrorism, New Zealand enjoyed a 30 percent increase in tourists over the same period.

So why should the Olympics reduce tourism? A possible explanation is that focus on the games undermines other forms of promotional spending, thus decreasing the appeal of the destination. After all, Greece and Australia have much more to offer than sporting events, but amid the noise of the Olympics, this fact was less easy to recognize. Boosters claim that an event such as the Olympics showcases the host city and the nation, but maybe it just focuses attention on a narrow range of interests, to the exclusion of everything else.

In the end, all of this comes down to a commonsense observation: hosting an event like the Olympic Games is like hosting a big party—whoever heard of getting rich from throwing a party? The boosters point out that the economy of a city or a nation is not like the economy of a household. That's true, but many of the same issues apply. Hosting a big party, I could spend a lot of money smartening up my home and impressing my friends, but that won't generate income. I might make good contacts that might subsequently turn into real income. But many other things would also have to happen before the cost of the party would be covered.

"What about the expense accounts of businesses?" the Olympics boosters ask. It's true, most big companies spend a lot of money on corporate hospitality, and much of this expense may contribute to winning business and therefore generating income in the future, but the connection is tenuous. If you went to the bank to ask for a $10,000 loan to wine and dine potential clients for your business, you would discover how little value is attributed to such spending.

These harsh facts of life come as a huge surprise to many people. Pro-sports optimists point to the studies carried out on behalf of governments to justify public spending on hosting a major sporting event. Such studies amount to a minor industry in their own right, with a full study costing something in the region of $100,000. Authors of these studies are understandably eager to reach conclusions that will please their clients. Unlike Enron, however, there is little chance that the consultant will be found out after the event. In fact, very few hosts conduct any post-event research. After the event, the boosters suddenly learn some good economics and say the correct yardstick is what would have happened without the games. Tourist numbers fell? Well, the fall would have been even bigger without the games! Since it is so intrinsically difficult to estimate economic impacts, the politicians see no need, and certainly no benefit, from raking over the past.

There is, however, a small community of economists dedicated to trying to measure impact after the event. These scholars are rather heroic, since their dedication to the truth makes them unwelcome in the lucrative consultancy jobs handed out by potential host cities. In order to try to pin down effects, these researchers make comparisons with similar cities that did not host the event. For example, one study looked at economic growth in major U.S. cities before, during, and after the 1994 World Cup. If cities that hosted games received an economic boost, they should have registered faster economic growth than cities that did not host games. In fact, the study found no statistically significant effect. There are a number of these studies, and almost all of them point in the same direction—there is no measurable economic gain in hosting a major event, and in many cases there is an economic loss.

One feature of most of these studies is that the event in question is too small in economic terms to make the significant impact so often claimed by the boosters. Greece was unusual in being the smallest economy since Finland in 1952 to host the summer games. $10 billion may be 5 percent of Greek GDP, but amounts to only one-tenth of 1 percent of U.S. GDP. The chance that the Atlanta games in 1996 posted any significant impact on the U.S. economy is remote. Barcelona is often cited as an example of a city that managed to relaunch its image on the back of the Olympics, but careful studies have shown that the city's rebirth was part of the redevelopment that began when Spain entered the European Union in 1986. Many of the facilities built for the Olympics have had a limited afterlife, and most of the construction projects that have changed the face of the city had little to do with the games.

This illustrates a very important point, what we might call "sporting money illusion." Sport seems very important to many of us, and thinking about it takes up a large percentage of our time. This fact can lead to the mistaken impression that sport has a larger monetary significance than it really does. Relative to the sums of money we spend on food, clothing, housing, health care, and the other essentials of life, what we spend on sports is negligible. This does not mean that sport is not important. In fact, one of the good things about sport is that we can get so much enjoyment from something that costs so little (a fact worth remembering when we complain about the price of a ticket). In many ways sport is like countryside— it surrounds us all and costs little or nothing to enjoy. However, this also means that the economic impact of sport (as opposed to its social and personal impact) is usually quite small.

None of this means that we should never pay to host major sporting events. Parties can be fun, even if they are costly. Likewise, there is nothing wrong in principle with governments deciding to subsidize an event such as the Olympic Games. Barcelona 1992 can be interpreted as a celebration of the rejuvenation of the city that had already taken place, just as China used Beijing 2008 as a way of underlining the country's arrival on the global stage. However, once it is recognized that the games impose an economic cost rather than a benefit, the problem of choice becomes a little tougher. Politicians and boosters present the case for hosting an event as "something for nothing": a big party that pays for itself. Who would say no to that? Once the true economic cost is recognized, the question becomes whether a party is the best use of taxpayers' money, or whether some alternative investment is preferable. Once politicians declare that there is $10 billion available to spend on a party, it doesn't take long for people to think of lots of good alternatives.

One way and another, governments spend quite a lot of money these days on sport. Besides funding specific events or building facilities, governments fund the training of elite athletes for events such as the Olympics. They also fund mass participation in sports, both in schools and in the community. Working out exactly how much of the government budget is spent on sport is difficult because the expenditure tends to be spread across a number of different government agencies and combined with a number of related activities such as education.

The origin of government spending on sport lies with the military. As was mentioned in chapter 1, although sport in Britain and the United States emerged largely as a private activity, in countries such as France and Germany the state backed the development of gymnastics and athletics in order to prepare young men for war. Even when sport was not seen as a preparation for war, there has been a close connection between sporting achievement and the military. The armed forces have always welcomed the prestige associated with employing elite athletes, and this is still true today. In the 2000 Sydney Olympic Games, 193 of the 927 medals awarded were won by members of the armed forces, that is, over one-fifth of the total. Since the vast majority of Olympic athletes nowadays are paid professionals, it seems a safe bet that no other profession is as well represented. Back in the 1960s and 1970s, when athletes were supposed to be amateurs, the proportion of military Olympic medal winners was about 25 percent, and in the 1980 Moscow games the proportion of soldier medalists was just under 40 percent. Those games were boycotted by the United States and dominated by the Communist countries. Those countries quite explicitly used sporting success as a way of spreading their political ideology and convincing others of their military might. The Western democracies may be a little less explicit in drawing this connection, but there is little doubt that "national prestige" has now replaced military readiness as the prime motive for government funding of elite sport. This is precisely how organizations such as the IOC and FIFA, despite widespread allegations of corruption and embezzlement, manage to retain their command over national governments. No one dares to offend institutions that have the power to deliver the world's most popular sporting events.

In essence this is a problem of monopoly. In the United States the major league sports franchises have in recent years found a similar way to exploit their monopoly power. During the early years of professional sports, team owners would build their own stadiums. However, once it became clear that there was a shortage of major league teams, owners no longer saw the need to pay for stadiums out of their own pockets. The trend was set back in 1953 when the Boston Braves moved to Milwaukee to take up residence in a stadium built for them at the expense of the local taxpayers (this was not the first stadium to be built at taxpayer expense, but it was the first that was used to tempt a franchise to move from one city to another). While the major leagues have increased the number of teams, there remain enough cities in the United States that would like to have a major league team to ensure that there will always be a healthy competition to build a stadium. A team doesn't even have to leave town; merely the threat is often enough to extort a subsidy from the incumbent city. Over the last twenty years there have been more than sixty publicly financed stadiums and arenas built in the United States at a cost of more than $20 billion. Most major league franchises have been provided with a new stadium at the expense of local taxpayers. For example, the cost of the stadium that brought a major league baseball team back to Washington, DC in 2004 (the Senators left in 1971) is now estimated to be $700 million.

All of the same kinds of arguments that are used to justify the Olympics are trotted out to justify stadium subsidies: they will create jobs, attract tourists, grow the local economy, and so on. In fact, these arguments are even less plausible than those we've heard about the Olympics. Most of the spending on the stadium (construction costs, player salaries) goes to people who live *outside* the city, and therefore the economic benefit is exported. Conversely, most of those who buy tickets live *inside* the city, and hence their spending is simply displacing leisure spending that would have gone to other local businesses. Again, there is little or no evidence that there are more jobs or more wealth in cities with franchises than in those without them.

This does not mean that nobody benefits from the construction of a new stadium. In fact, a stadium brings a lot of benefits to the team owner. First, new stadiums enjoy a honeymoon effect in terms of attendance, with more fans coming to games. One reason is that a new stadium often offers a better experience for the fans (as well as more opportunities to spend money). Another reason is that teams with new stadiums experience a surge in success in the first few years. This may be because of increased support for the team, but may also be because the owner invests more in talent, either because they expect a better return or because it was part of the deal that got the stadium built in the first place.

All this translates into a significant revenue boost for whoever has the right to charge for admission. Despite the fact that many stadiums are built at public expense, the owner of the franchise typically retains the right to all of the revenue generated, and usually this is not merely from ticket sales, but also highly profitable car-parking revenues. Some economists have estimated that the boost in income following the construction of a new stadium is large enough to cover the capital costs. In other words, even without a subsidy, owners could pay for the stadium themselves and still make a profit. No wonder it is hard to credit the owners of franchises who claim that their teams lose money.

Many of these economic truths have been understood for many years, perhaps by a majority of the voting public, but the stadium subsidy bandwagon rolls on regardless. One way that critics hit upon to try and stop it was the referendum. From the 1980s a significant fraction of subsidy proposals were put to the vote, and a significant fraction were turned down. However, more than 50 percent were approved. This is perhaps not surprising, since many voters will be at least as desperate as the politicians to have a major league team, and there will be a tendency for those who care most to be most likely to vote. Moreover, if voters understand the honeymoon effect, then they may have good reason to vote for subsidy. However, many economists have pointed out the regressive nature of these subsidies, usually paid out of a sales tax, which hits poorer people hardest, while those who can afford to buy tickets tend to come from the higher income brackets. Fundamentally, a local referendum cannot in itself overturn the monopoly power of the major leagues.

A striking contrast to this situation is provided by the English Premier League, one of the biggest and most successful soccer leagues in the world. Between 1993 and

2002 clubs spent $3 billion on new stadiums and stadium refurbishment, but benefited from a public subsidy amounting to only 10 percent or so of the total. In part this has to do with limitations on the spending powers of local government in England, but it is also a function of the structure of the leagues. The open league system, where major and minor leagues are connected in a hierarchy through promotion and relegation, effectively negates the relocation threat. Anyone can start a team in any city, and if the team employs good enough players, it can be promoted up the leagues to the highest level. This is not merely a theoretical possibility—over a period of years many small teams are promoted from three of four tiers below the top level (even from amateur or semi-pro status) up to the highest level. Likewise, some top teams have been known to sink three of four levels down the hierarchy. Thus there is no need for a city to persuade a team to move in order to reach the highest level of play. Indeed, franchise mobility is largely prohibited within the soccer system. The promotion and relegation system ensures that a fixed set of teams cannot obtain a monopoly over "major league" play, and hence the kind of blackmail used in the United States is unknown.

This is not to say that governments do not subsidize stadiums. Practice varies by country. In most of Europe, sports clubs have developed largely with the financial backing of the state, primarily for the purpose of providing sport and physical education for those who want to participate. For example, in Germany there exists a network of clubs, or *Vereine* (which developed out of the nineteenth-century Turnen gymnastic clubs) where members pay a fee. Subsidies are also provided by local government, particularly for capital projects that might include stadium construction. Many of the top German soccer teams remain part of these clubs to the present day. Yet nowadays the bigger clubs fund their own stadium development out of membership fees, ticket sales, and revenue from broadcast rights. Even when Germany hosted the 2006 World Cup less than half of the cost of stadium construction and refurbishment came from the public sector. However, in other countries public subsidies can be much larger. For example, the stadiums constructed in Italy for the 1990 World Cup were largely funded by local government, which continues to own many of these facilities. This is a mixed blessing for many of these clubs, since frequently the local government also controls ticket pricing, and holds down prices to buy political popularity.

One feature that emerges from these stories is that public subsidies are motivated by the popularity politicians expect to win from them. This leads politicians to focus on big payoffs, such as attracting a major event or bringing a major league team to town. Moreover, organizers of big events and owners of sports franchises have understood the political process and have succeeded in creating competition for what they sell, so that they can extract ever-bigger subsidies. Is this the best use of public money? One answer is that if this is what the public wants, then they are entitled to have it. Indeed, notwithstanding all the economic arguments, there is good evidence that citizens want and are willing to pay for the right to host a major event or team, and therefore we should not be too quick to dismiss such spending as waste.

There is, however, a downside. Government budgets are not unlimited, and spending on one activity reduces the available budget for others. Spending public money on goods and services that are essentially for private consumption is wasteful in the sense that consumers and businesses would pay for these costs anyway. Even the Olympic Games, if managed on a less lavish scale, could pay their own way. There are some goods and services that would never be able to pay their own way, and yet may be socially valuable and deserving of public investment. These goods tend to be those that produce "externalities," that is, benefits that do not directly accrue exclusively to the immediate recipient, and therefore cannot be charged directly to that person. Education is a good example: we all benefit from the education of young people, since their being able to do things such as read and write benefits the rest of us. Educated people can hold down good jobs and raise the standard of living in our society, which can benefit all of us. Public subsidy for education is a way all of us contribute to the benefit that we receive from the education of others.

The participation of young people in sports also produces externalities that can benefit all of us. The evidence shows that participation at a young age tends to lead to a more active lifestyle in later years. A more active population is more productive and generates more wealth for society as a whole and places less demands on the health system. These benefits can be paid for through public subsidy of sports facilities in schools and in parks. However, this requires substantial investment, particularly in areas of social and economic deprivation. It also requires a culture that values the efforts of everyone, rather than the Olympian achievements of a few. While politicians pay lip service to these principles, their interest in subsidizing the big prestige projects leads to underfunding of more useful activities. In passing, it should be noted that no one has yet been able to demonstrate that hosting an event such as the Olympics does anything to increase participation in sports. From militarism to national and local jingoism, the involvement of government in sport has often done more harm than good. Ensuring that public funds are spent in the right way has always been a problem, and one that is likely to remain into the future.

EPILOGUE

Modern sports are undoubtedly in a mess. Corruption, exploitation, monopoly abuse, drug abuse, cheating, foul conduct on the field and criminal offenses off it—there is almost no form of human misconduct that cannot be found in abundance. If the old adage that sport is a mirror of society is true, then there is much that we should be ashamed to see. Yet sports have never been more popular than they are today. All of the abuses that we see are a consequence of our own intense desire to watch our own team, our own country, or our favored athlete win. We want to see excess, we want the contest to be taken to the ultimate limit, and we are willing to pay handsomely for it. Our demand for winning is what drives much of the excess in the sports world of today. Athletes who take drugs and managers who turn a blind eye to criminal offenses are merely competing to meet our demands. Clubs that raise ticket prices and blackmail cities to build them stadiums at taxpayers' expense are only responding to the profit incentives that our demand for winning creates. One could even argue that officials who accept bribes in exchange for the right to host major events are ensuring that those who value these rights most win them, a standard condition for economic efficiency.

While it is possible for economists and other social analysts to explain and provide insights into the causes of bad behavior, relatively few prescriptions are likely to change the undesirable climate we all observe. Our addiction to winning is the source of the problem. Moreover, the possibility for winners to reach an ever-increasing fraction of the global population through technology has increased the value of winning to unprecedented levels. One thing seems sure: the excesses of today will be dwarfed by the malfeasance that is to come.

Some people argue that more government regulation is the answer: regulate ticket prices, control wages, and punish drug cheats with prison sentences. Yet this would attack the symptoms rather than the disease. Moreover, the influence of government is likely to lead to greater distortions and misallocations, as the last chapter should have amply demonstrated. To deal with the root of the problem we have to go back to the origins of modern sports. It wasn't always like this. When the Knickerbocker Club of New York laid down the rules of baseball, it did so in the desire to share with others the fellowship and good spirit engendered by participation in their game. It may seem hard to believe, but winning was not that important. Much the same was true of the gentlemen cricketers of England or the gymnastic Turners in Germany, who, for the most part, were in fact more interested in beer drinking than the military exercises advocated by their more ideological leaders. Modern sport grew first and foremost out of sociability. Even today, there are many professional sportsmen from the past who bemoan the loss of sociability in sport caused by the growing importance of money. Professionalism itself helped drive sociability out of sport. But professionalism was in turn driven by the demand to watch, and ultimately the demand to watch one's favorite team win.

This is not to say that the world of the gentleman amateur was perfect or even admirable. Sociability often meant socializing with a certain kind of person, to the exclusion of others considered inferior, whether in economic wealth, social standing, race, creed, or gender. Nonetheless, the demand for winning has driven the gentler virtues out of modern sport, and this demand comes from those of us who watch and enjoy sport.

Is there anything that can be done? Modern fans often feel a despair brought on by the Hobson's choice with which they are presented: either give up the sport altogether (and many fans do turn their backs in disgust) or connive at the continuing excesses on and off the field. At root there is a problem of collective action: individually each of us is powerless to change events, while collectively it is our willingness to stick with sport that creates the problem. However, as is often the case, there are some feedback mechanisms that may temper the excesses of the future. An important trend in broadcasting has been the growth of channel capacity, created by digital broadcasting and developments in cable and satellite technologies. Increasingly, channel capacity has fragmented audiences.

Another important source of fragmentation is the globalization of sport and the rising economic power of the world's most populous nations, China and India. The Beijing Olympic Games in 2008 were controversial in North America and Europe for their political overtones, but there was no doubting the enthusiasm of ordinary Chinese people for sport, and as their economic power grows, they will surely develop their own championships. Perhaps an even more important harbinger of change was the foundation of the Indian Premier League. This new cricket competition was started in 2008, building on a new, shorter competitive format called Twenty20, which takes about as long to play as a baseball game. The competition organizers also used the American franchise model to raise $800 million from business tycoons interested in running a team, and over $1 billion from Sony for the broadcasting rights. Along with cheerleaders, loud music, and other forms of modern razzmatazz, the competition took the nation by storm, mainly because the money raised had been used to bring together the world's best cricketers. The success of the competition signaled the dominance of Indian economic muscle in this sport, leaving traditional fans in countries such as the UK and Australia largely out in the cold.

If all this means that sports fans are spreading their affections over a wider range of activities, then likewise the biggest events are starting to see their audiences diminish. People may watch more sports, but each sport receives a smaller share of the total attention of consumers. If the big leagues start to receive a smaller share of our attention, perhaps the importance of winning might diminish just a little, and allow some space for other virtues to show themselves on the field of play.

A Beginner's Guide to the Sports Economics Literature

In this guide there are specific references for each chapter, but first it may be useful for readers to have a general overview. The study of sports economics is still in its infancy, but it already has its classics. The year 2006 saw the fiftieth anniversary of an analysis that by common consent is both the first paper in the literature and still one of the best: Simon Rottenberg, "The Baseball Player's Labor Market," *Journal of Political Economy* 64 (1956): 242–58. Its importance lies in its careful discussion of how playing talent will be distributed in a market in which team owners maximize profit and act independently, resulting in Rottenberg's statement of the "invariance principle" (discussed in chapter 3). The invariance principle bears a strong resemblance to the well-known Coase theorem (Ronald Coase, "The Problem of Social Cost," *Journal of Law and Economics* 3 [1960]: 1–44). A more lighthearted but frequently insightful paper is Walter Neale, "The Peculiar Economics of Professional Sport," *Quarterly Journal of Economics* 78, no. 1 (1964): 1–14.

The first papers to treat the economics of sport from a European perspective were by Peter Sloane: "The Labour Market in Professional Football," *British Journal of Industrial Relations* 7, no. 2 (1969): 81–99, and "The Economics of Professional Football: The Football Club as a Utility Maximiser," *Scottish Journal of Political Economy* 17, no. 2 (1971): 121–46. Given the presumption that American team owners maximize profits while many European professional sports clubs have not-for-profit status, there is a substantial literature on whether there exists a distinct

European model of sport. See, for example, Stefan Szymanski, "Is There a European Model of Sport?" in *International Sports Economics*, edited by R. Fort and J. Fizel (Praeger, 2004). The debate has drawn in the politicians (see, for example, European Commission, "The European Model of Sport," consultation paper of DGX, 1998), fearful that an American culture will supplant the indigenous strain; see Thomas Hoehn and Stefan Szymanski, "The Americanization of European Football," *Economic Policy* 28 (1999): 205–40. This concern is often related to the question of the financial stability of European sport; see the special issue on the financial crisis in European football, *Journal of Sports Economics* 7 (2006).

The seminal paper on contests was written by Gordon Tullock in the 1960s, "Efficient Rent Seeking," reprinted in *Toward a Theory of Rent-Seeking Society*, edited by J. Buchanan, R. Tollison, and G. Tullock (Texas A&M University Press, 1980), 97–112. Unfortunately Tullock was not much interested in the application of his model to sports, and until recently those who wrote about sports economics did not explore the apparatus developed by Tullock. The first formal economic model of a sports league was Mohamed El-Hodiri and James Quirk, "An Economic Model of a Professional Sports League," *Journal of Political Economy* 79 (1971): 1302–19. Other contributions in this vein are summarized by Rodney Fort and James Quirk, "Cross Subsidization, Incentives and Outcomes in Professional Team Sports Leagues," *Journal of Economic Literature* 33, no. 3 (1995): 1265–99, and John Vrooman, "A General Theory of Professional Sports Leagues," *Southern Economic Journal* 61, no. 4 (1995): 971–90. However, papers that followed this tradition eschewed a game-theoretic approach, leading to a significant critique by

Stefan Szymanski and Stefan Késenne, "Competitive Balance and Gate Revenue Sharing in Team Sports," *Journal of Industrial Economics* 52, no. 1 (2004): 165–77. In essence the debate in this literature can be summarized in one simple question—will the distribution of talent that results from competition among team owners under the rules of the league be the same as the distribution that would maximize total profits for the owners and total welfare for consumers (and if not, how would these allocations differ)? This question has stimulated both an intense theoretical debate and a rich empirical literature examining the impact of arrangements such as the reserve clause, free agency, and draft rules. See, for example, Daniel Marburger, "Property Rights and Unilateral Player Transfers in a Multiconference Sports League," *Journal of Sports Economics* 3, no. 2 (2002): 122–32, and Craig Depken, "Free-Agency and the Competitiveness of Major League Baseball," *Review of Industrial Organization* 14 (1999): 205–17.

The first paper to show how performance and pay in sports could be linked empirically was Gerald Scully, "Pay and Performance in Major League Baseball," *American Economic Review* 64 (1974): 915–30. It spawned significant developments in the literature. First, it might be argued that this paper was the progenitor of the sports productivity literature, reviewed in Lawrence Kahn, "The Sports Business as a Labor Market Laboratory," *Journal of Economic Perspectives* 14, no. 3 (2000): 75–94. This literature is also closely related to the work of the founder of Sabermetrics, Bill James (see *The New Bill James Historical Baseball Abstract* [Free Press, 2003]). This line of research can also claim to be the root of Billy Beane's work on identifying value for money and baseball batters, memorably portrayed in the best-selling book by Michael Lewis, *Moneyball*. Second, if productivity can be measured and compared against wages paid, it is possible to test whether some groups are systematically under- or overpaid, that is, to test for discrimination. Developments of the Scully model have been used to test discrimination against African Americans in baseball (Clark Nardinelli and Curtis Simon, "Customer Racial Discrimination in the Market for Memorabilia: The Case of Baseball," *Quarterly Journal of Economics* 105 [1990]: 575–95), and against French Canadians in ice hockey (J.C.H. Jones, S. Nadeau, and W. D. Walsh, "Ethnicity, Productivity and Salary: Player Compensation and Discrimination in the National Hockey League," *Applied Economics* 23 [1999]: 179–86).

The first proper survey of the major themes in sports economics can be found in Roger Noll, editor, *Government and the Sports Business* (Brookings Institution Press, 1974). Economists have had a patchy record of involvement in the formulation of public policy toward sports (sadly, most economists feel the issue is not "serious" enough to merit their attention; one wonders what Plato or Aristotle, who wrote about the role of athletic exercise in citizenship, would have said). Rottenberg was inspired by his involvement with the Celler Committee hearings in Congress, but since the U.S. government has largely steered clear of involvement in sports, so have most American public policy analysts. Honorable exceptions include Roger Noll, who has maintained his involvement over four decades; James Quirk and Rodney Fort, in *Hard Ball: The Abuse of Power in Pro Team Sports* (Princeton University Press, 1999); and Andrew Zimbalist, *May the Best Team Win* (Brookings Institution Press, 2003). Moreover, one or two lawyers have trespassed into the reserve of economists and made important contributions to the public policy debate, notably Gary Roberts, "Sports Leagues and the Sherman Act: The Use and Abuse of Section 1 to Regulate Restraints on Intraleague Rivalry," *UCLA Law Review* 32 (1984): 219–87; Stephen F. Ross, "Monopoly Sports Leagues," *Minnesota Law Review* 73 (1989): 643–761; and Stephen F. Ross and Stefan Szymanski, *Fans of the World, Unite! A (Capitalist) Manifesto for Sports Consumers* (Stanford University Press, 2008).

In recent years the sports economics literature has grown so fast that a newcomer to the field would do well to seek out some overviews at the beginning. There are now a couple of useful textbooks: Rodney Fort, *Sports Economics*, 2nd edition (Prentice Hall, 2006), and Michael Leeds and Peter von Allmen, *The Economics of Sports*, 3rd edition (Addison-Wesley, 2007), both of which focus almost exclusively on the United States, and Robert Sandy, Peter Sloane, and Mark Rosentraub, *The Economics of Sports: An International Perspective* (Palgrave, 2004). There are also popular books introducing general issues, such as David J. Berri, Martin B. Schmidt, and Stacey L. Brook, *The Wages of Wins: Taking Measure of the Many Myths in Modern Sport* (Stanford University Press, 2006), and J. C. Bradbury, *The Baseball Economist* (Dutton Adult, 2007). For a very brief introduction to most topics in sports economics a useful reference is Wladimir Andreff and Stefan Szymanski, editors, *Handbook on the Economics of Sport* (Edward Elgar, 2006).

Chapter 1

The classic investigation of the role of sport in modern society is Johan Huizinga, *Homo Ludens: A Study of the Play Element in Culture* (Beacon Press, 1955), while the classic statement about the role of sociability in the emergence of modern society is Jürgen Habermas, *The Structural Transformation of the Public Sphere* (Polity Press, 1989). An eclectic sociological study of the diffusion of modern sports is Allen Guttman, *Games and Empires: Modern Sports and Cultural Imperialism* (Columbia University Press, 1994). The role of sport in Britain since the Industrial Revolution is analyzed by Richard Holt, *Sport and the British* (Oxford University Press, 1989). The development of team sports in America is documented by George Kirsch, *The Creation of American Team Sports* (University of Illinois Press, 1989). A detailed comparison of the evolution of professional baseball and soccer is to be found in Stefan Szymanski and Andrew Zimbalist, *National Pastime* (Brookings Institution Press, 2005).

Chapter 2

The fundamentals of contest theory as applied to sport are explored in Stefan Szymanski, "The Economic Design of Sporting Contests," *Journal of Economic Literature* 41 (2003): 1137–87. There has been disagreement about the appropriate objectives to assume when analyzing the behavior of clubs in sports leagues, and this is discussed extensively in Wladimir Andreff and Paul Staudohar, "The Evolving Model of European Sports Finance," *Journal of Sports Economics* 1, no. 3 (2000): 257–76; Stefan Késenne, "League Management in Professional Team Sports with Win Maximizing Clubs," *European Journal for Sport Management* 2, no. 2 (1996): 14–22; and Stefan Késenne, "The Impact of Salary Caps in Professional Team Sports," *Scottish Journal of Political Economy* 47, no. 4 (2000): 422–30.

The analysis of promotion and relegation is considered in Roger Noll, "The Economics of Promotion and Relegation in Sports Leagues: The Case of English Football," *Journal of Sports Economics* 3, no. 2 (2002): 169–203; Stephen F. Ross and Stefan Szymanski, "Open Competition in League Sports," *Wisconsin Law Review* 2002: 625–56; and Stefan Szymanski and Tommaso Valletti, "Promotion and Relegation in Sporting Contests," *Rivista di Politica Economica*, December 2005, 3–49.

Chapter 3

The issue of demand for attendance and the uncertainty-of-outcome hypothesis is surveyed in Jeffery Borland and Robert Macdonald, "Demand for Sport," *Oxford Review of Economic Policy* 19, no. 4 (2003): 478–502. The relationship between budgets and winning is considered in Stefan Szymanski and Ron Smith, "The English Football Industry: Profit, Performance and Industrial Structure," *International Review of Applied Economics* 11, no. 1 (1997): 135–53; Stephen Hall, Stefan Szymanski, and Andrew Zimbalist, "Testing Causality between Team Performance and Payroll: The Cases of Major League Baseball and English Soccer," *Journal of Sports Economics* 3, no. 2 (2002): 149–68; and David Forrest and Robert Simmons, "Team Salaries and Playing Success in Sports: A Comparative Perspective," *Zeitschrift für Betriebswirtschaft* 72, no. 4 (2002): 221–36. The legality of restraints in sports leagues under the competition law is dealt with by Alan Balfour and Philip Porter, "The Reserve Clause in Professional Sports: Legality and Effect on Competitive Balance," *Labor Law Journal* 42 (1991): 8–18; Michael Flynn and Richard

192 SPORTS ECONOMICS LITERATURE

Gilbert, "An Analysis of Professional Sports Leagues as Joint Ventures," *Economic Journal* 111 (2001): F27–F46; Gary Roberts, "Sports Leagues and the Sherman Act: The Use and Abuse of Section 1 to Regulate Restraints on Intraleague Rivalry," *UCLA Law Review* 32 (1984): 219–87; and Stephen F. Ross, "Monopoly Sports Leagues," *Minnesota Law Review* 73 (1989): 643–761. A European perspective can be found in Stefan Késenne and Claude Jeanrenaud, editors, *Competition Policy in Professional Sports: Europe after the Bosman Case* (Antwerp Standaard Editions, 1999). Studies of measures to enhance competitive balance include Kevin Grier and Robert Tollison, "The Rookie Draft and Competitive Balance: The Case of Professional Football," *Journal of Economic Behavior and Organization* 25 (1994): 293–98. An interesting perspective on competitive balance and team production can be found in David J. Berri, Martin B. Schmidt, and Stacey L. Brook, *The Wages of Wins: Taking Measure of the Many Myths in Modern Sport* (Stanford University Press, 2006).

Chapter 4

On sporting incentives and the labor market see Ronald Ehrenberg and Michael Bognanno, "Do Tournaments Have Incentive Effects?" *Journal of Political Economy* 98, no. 6 (1990): 1307–24; B. Frick and J. Prinz, "Pay and Performance in Professional Road Running: The Case of City Marathons," Department of Economics, University of Witten/Herdecke, 2002; Lawrence Kahn, "Managerial Quality, Team Success, and Individual Performance in Major League Baseball," *Industrial and Labor Relations Review* 46 (1993): 531–47; Sherwin Rosen, "The Economics of Superstars," *American Economic Review* 71 (1981): 845–58; Sherwin Rosen and Allen Sanderson, "Labor Markets in Professional Sports," *Economic Journal* 111, no. 469 (2001): F47–F68; and Paul Staudohar, *Playing for Dollars: Labor Relations and the Sports Business* (ILR Press, 1996). On Moneyball, see Jahn K. Hakes and Raymond D. Sauer, "An Economic Evaluation of the *Moneyball* Hypothesis," *Journal of Economic Perspectives* 20, no. 3 (2006): 173–86. On cheating in sumo see Steven Levitt and Stephen Dubner, *Freakonomics* (Penguin, 2005). For biases among officials see Neil Rickman and Robert Witt, "Favoritism and Financial Incentives: A Natural Experiment," *Economica* 75, no. 298 (2008): 296–309 (soccer); Joseph Price and Justin Wolfers, "Racial Discrimination among NBA Referees," NBER Working Paper 13206, 2007 (basketball); and Christopher A. Parsons, Johan Sulaeman, Michael C. Yates, and Daniel S. Hamermesh, "Strike Three: Umpires' Demand for Discrimination," NBER Working Paper 13665, 2007 (baseball).

Chapter 5

On sport and broadcasting, see Martin Cave and Robert W. Crandall, "Sports Rights and the Broadcast Industry," *Economic Journal* 111 (2001): F4–F26; C. Cowie and M. Williams, "The Economics of Sports Rights," *Telecommunications Policy* 21, no. 7 (1997): 619–34; David Forrest, Rob Simmons, and Stefan Szymanski, "Broadcasting, Attendance and the Inefficiency of Cartels," *Review of Industrial Organization* 24 (2004): 243–65; and Tom Hoehn and David Lancefield, "Broadcasting and Sport," *Oxford Review of Economic Policy* 19, no. 4 (2003): 552–68. An influential paper that gives insights into how competition for pay-TV rights operates is M. Armstrong, "Competition in the Pay-TV Market," *Journal of the Japanese and International Economies* 13 (1999): 257–80.

Chapter 6

Here is a roll call of some of the hero-economists who have dispassionately reported the evidence on the impact of major sporting events, without fear or favor, often suffering personal abuse, and frequently denying themselves the opportunity to line their own pockets for the price of saying what the politicians would like to hear: R. Baade, "Professional Sports as Catalysts for Metropolitan Economic Development," *Journal of Urban Affairs* 18, no. 1 (1996): 1–17; R. Baade and V. Matheson, "Bidding for the Olympics: Fool's Gold?" in Carlos Barros, Muradali Ibrahimo, and Stefan Szymanski, editors, *Transatlantic Sport* (Edward Elgar, 2002); R. Baade and V. Matheson, "The Quest for the Cup: Assessing the Economic Impact of the World Cup," working paper, 2002; J. Crompton, "Economic Impact Analysis of Sports Facilities and Events: Eleven Sources of Misapplication," *Journal of Sport Management* 9, no. 1 (1995): 14–35; Roger Noll and Andrew Zimbalist, editors, *Sports, Jobs, and Taxes: The Economic Impact of Sports Teams and Stadiums* (Brookings Institution Press, 1997); Holger Preuss, *The Economics of Staging the Olympics: A Comparison of the Games, 1972–2008* (Edward Elgar, 2004); and John Siegfried and Andrew Zimbalist, "The Economics of Sports Facilities and Their Communities," *Journal of Economic Perspectives* 14 (2000): 95–114. In recent years new ways to estimate economic impacts have been developed—from the construction of large-scale computable general equilibrium models (see R. Madden, "The Economic Consequences of the Sydney Olympics: The CREA/Arthur Andersen Study," *Current Issues in Tourism* 5, no. 1 [2002]: 7–21), to hedonic regressions (see G. Carlino and N. E. Coulson, "Compensating Differentials and the Social Benefits of the NFL," *Journal of Urban Economics* 56, no. 1 [2004]: 25–50), to contingent valuation methods (B. K. Johnson, P. A. Groothuis, and J. C. Whitehead, "The Value of Public Goods Generated by a Major League Sports Team: The CVM Approach," *Journal of Sports Economics* 2, no. 1 [2002]: 6–21). A recent survey of contributions can be found in G. Kavetsos and Stefan Szymanski, "National Wellbeing and International Sports Events," *Journal of Economic Psychology*, forthcoming.

Acknowledgments

This book summarizes nearly twenty years of thinking about the economics of sports. I have accumulated a lot of intellectual and emotional debts in the process; I can repay only a few here, and not in full. I would like to thank my many sporting coauthors over the years: Kevin Alavy, Wladimir Andreff, Tunde Buraimo, Giles Atkinson, Luigi Buzzacchi, David Forrest, Filippo dell'Osso, Pedro Garcia-del-Barrio, Steve Hall, David Harbord, Takeo Hirata, Tom Hoehn, Georgios Kavetsos, Stefan Késenne, Tim Kuypers, Umberto Lago, Stephanie Leach, Neil Longley, Susana Mourato, Susanne Parlasca, Ian Preston, Steve Ross, Rob Simmons, Ron Smith, Tommaso Valletti, and Andy Zimbalist. Then there are all the other sports economists who have given me valuable comments and feedback over the years, too many to mention by name but each one a contributor to this book.

This book would never have seen the light of day without Seth Ditchik from Princeton University Press, who suggested it in the first place and saw it through to publication. Peter Allden generously read through the entire manuscript and made many very useful suggestions. I also thank Ellen Foos and Jennifer Roth and the staff at Princeton for dealing with the manuscript promptly and efficiently, and Richard Isomaki for his careful copyediting.

Index

and, 9–11; power of, 13; private schools and, 14; professionalism and, 94; promotion and, 56–58; reserve rule and, 73–91; salary levels and, 94–95; sociological analysis of, 9–10; stadium building and, 175–77; television and, 125; vertical separation and, 51–56. *See also* leagues
coaches: broadcasting and, 25; drug use and, 122; motivation by, 112–13; technology and, 137; underperformance and, 117–18; winning and, 28
Coase, Ronald, xix, 185
Coase Theorem, 82–83
coffeehouses, 11
collective bargaining, 83–84
collective decision-making, 54–56
collective selling, xii–xiv, 88–89, 133–34, 146–48, 182
Comiskey, Charles, 119
Commerce Committee, 158–59
commercialism: amateur model and, 2–3, 25–26; antitrust and, 59–91 (*see* also antitrust); broadcasting and, 146–47 (*see also* broadcasting); business model of, 21–22; clubs and, 20, 22; competitive balance defense and, 73–91; development of, 20–22; entertainment and, 28; FIFA and, 24;

fraud in, 156–58; merchandising and, 85, 94, 100, 140, 159; monopolies and, 51–56 (*see also* monopolies); Olympics and, 22, 156–58; optimal league size and, 33; organizers and, 27–58; as profane, 20–21; profit motives and, 33–35; promotion and, 56–58; Sarbanes-Oxley Act and, 156–57; soccer and, 22–24; telephone companies and, 36
commissioners, 33: antitrust and, 80, 87; blackouts and, 138; Blue Ribbon Panel on Baseball Economics and, 87; broadcasting and, 132, 138–39; collective decision-making and, 55–56; competitive balance defense and, 80; revenue and, 132
competition: alternative structures and, 36–43; amateur model and, 25; antitrust and, 59–91 (*see also* antitrust); balance and, 138, 192; broadcasting and, 125, 144–45, 151–53; cheating and, 27–28, 56 (*see also* cheating); collective selling and, xii–xiv, 88–89, 133–34, 146–48; contribution to total effort and, 30–31; drugs and, 44, 92–93, 98, 122–24, 180; effort levels

DATE DUE

DEC 0 7 2010			
DEC 2 2 2011			
DEC 1 3 2013			
MELCAT			
JUN 2014			

Demco, Inc. 38-293

MARK & HELEN OSTERLIN LIBRARY
NORTHWESTERN MICHIGAN COLLEGE
TRAVERSE CITY, MICHIGAN 49686-3061